BATTLES
THAT CHANGED THE WORLD

FIRST BATTLE OF THE MARNE

GETTYSBURG

HASTINGS

MARATHON

MIDWAY

NORMANDY

SARATOGA

TENOCHTITLAN

TET OFFENSIVE

WATERLOO

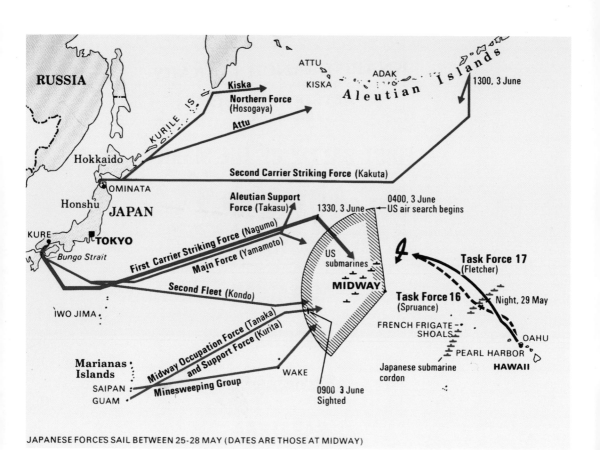

RUSSIA

ATTU
KISKA
ADAK
Aleutian Islands
1300, 3 June

Kiska
Northern Force
(Hosogaya)

Attu

KURILE IS.

Hokkaido

Second Carrier Striking Force (Kakuta)

OMINATA

Honshu   JAPAN

Aleutian Support
Force (Takasu)

1330, 3 June

0400, 3 June
US air search begins

KURE

TOKYO

Bungo Strait

First Carrier Striking Force (Nagumo)

Main Force (Yamamoto)

US
submarines

MIDWAY

Task Force 17
(Fletcher)

Second Fleet (Kondo)

Task Force 16
(Spruance)

Night, 29 May

IWO JIMA

FRENCH FRIGATE
SHOALS

Marianas
Islands

Midway Occupation Force (Tanaka)
and Support Force (Kurita)

OAHU

PEARL HARBOR

SAIPAN

Minesweeping Group

WAKE

Japanese submarine
cordon

HAWAII

GUAM

0900 3 June
Sighted

JAPANESE FORCES SAIL BETWEEN 25-28 MAY (DATES ARE THOSE AT MIDWAY)

BATTLES
THAT CHANGED THE WORLD

MIDWAY

RICHARD WORTH

CHELSEA HOUSE PUBLISHERS
PHILADELPHIA

FRONTIS: These maps show the sequence of events and routes taken by the forces of the United States and Japan at the Battle of Midway.

COVER: U.S. Navy planes attacking Japanese targets.

CHELSEA HOUSE PUBLISHERS

EDITOR IN CHIEF Sally Cheney
DIRECTOR OF PRODUCTION Kim Shinners
CREATIVE MANAGER Takeshi Takahashi
MANUFACTURING MANAGER Diann Grasse

STAFF FOR MIDWAY

EDITOR Lee Marcott
PICTURE RESEARCHER Pat Burns
PRODUCTION ASSISTANT Jaimie Winkler
COVER AND SERIES DESIGNER Keith Trego
LAYOUT 21st Century Publishing and Communications, Inc.

http://www.chelseahouse.com

First Printing

1 3 5 7 9 8 6 4 2

Library of Congress Cataloging-in-Publication Data

Worth, Richard.
    Midway / Richard Worth.
          p. cm. --   (Battles that changed the world)
Includes bibliographical references and index.
    ISBN 0-7910-6686-X (hardcover) -- ISBN 0-7910-7111-1 (pbk.)
   1.   Midway, Battle of, 1942. 2.   World War, 1939-1945--Naval
operations, American. 3.   World War, 1939-1945--Naval operations,
Japanese. 4.   World War, 1939-1945--Campaigns--Pacific Ocean.   I.
Title.
II. Series.
   D774.M5 W67 2002
   940.54'5973--dc21

                                                              2002004119

CONTENTS

1 BREAKING THE CODE 7

2 THE RISING SUN 17

3 THE UNITED STATES
IN THE PACIFIC 29

4 JAPAN'S EARLY SUCCESSES 41

5 PREPARING FOR MIDWAY 55

6 THE BATTLE BEGINS 65

7 DESTROYING JAPANESE
AIRCRAFT CARRIERS 77

8 TURNING POINT IN THE PACIFIC 87

TIMELINE & CHRONOLOGY 96

FURTHER READING 99

INDEX 100

Breaking the Code

On December 7, 1941, the Japanese launched a surprise attack on Pearl Harbor, Hawaii. The USS *Arizona* was torpedoed and sunk in the attack.

On December 31, 1941, Admiral Chester W. Nimitz became commander in chief of the U.S. fleet in the Pacific Ocean. The tall, handsome, white-haired Nimitz was a career naval officer. Graduating from the Naval Academy at Annapolis, Maryland, in 1905, Nimitz served aboard a battleship and later on the staff of the commanding officer of America's Atlantic submarine fleet during World War I. Following the war, he commanded a cruiser and later he was put in charge of an entire division of battleships. Nimitz also became an enthusiastic supporter of building aircraft carriers—these new flattop ships that could launch planes against an enemy position were changing the style of naval warfare. By 1938, he had become a rear admiral and eventually he might expect to achieve a position like Pacific commander in chief (CINC-PAC). But when that promotion actually came, it could not have happened at a worse time.

Less than four weeks earlier, the United States had suffered the worst military defeat in its history. On the morning of December 7, 1941, the Japanese had launched a surprise attack on the important American naval base at Pearl Harbor, Hawaii. The strike occurred when the backbone of America's fleet—battleships, cruisers, and destroyers—were at anchor in the harbor. In less than two hours, waves of Japanese aircraft had decimated the fleet as well as crippled or destroyed over 200 Army planes on nearby airfields. Fortunately the American aircraft carriers were not at Pearl Harbor, but instead they were out on patrol, so they were spared.

By the time Nimitz took command, American forces in the Pacific were reeling. One of his immediate tasks was to restore morale at Pearl Harbor. He realized that the Navy had many fine officers who were in no way responsible for what had happened at Pearl. Nimitz reassured these men that he wanted them to work with him to recover the initiative in the Pacific. "It was like being in a stuffy room and having someone open a window and let in a breath of fresh air," said one officer.

Nimitz had also been charged with holding the line against Japan at the American positions in Hawaii and the Midway Islands. But it was a daunting task. The Japanese fleet far outnumbered the American fleet. Following the victory at Pearl Harbor, Japan had also captured a string of other positions, which made it supreme in the western Pacific. The American islands of Guam and Wake had fallen in December, followed by the capture of Hong Kong, the fall of the Dutch East Indies, and finally by the surrender of the American armies defending the

Admiral Chester W. Nimitz became the commander in chief of the Pacific Fleet on December 31, 1941. He was responsible for maintaining the American positions in Hawaii and the Midway Islands.

Philippines in May. Japanese planes even bombed Port Darwin on the northern coast of Australia.

One of the principal architects of Japanese victory was Admiral Isoroku Yamamoto. Known as the "Iron Admiral," Yamamoto was only five feet three inches tall.

He had spent his entire career in the Japanese navy. Yamamoto was a graduate of the Japanese naval academy at Etajima and later served on a Japanese cruiser. In 1919, Yamamoto went to Boston, Massachusetts, to study English and while there he became an excellent poker player, as well. He returned to Japan, becoming an expert on aerial warfare, which was transforming the role of both the army and navy. In 1926, Yamamoto was sent back to the United States as a naval attaché. During his years there, he developed a profound respect for America's industrial strength and military power. Yamamoto believed that it was foolish for Japan to go to war against the United States, which seemed far too powerful to be defeated. However, when Japanese leaders made the decision that conflict was inevitable, he threw himself into the task of preparing an effective naval strategy.

Admiral Yamamoto had developed the strategy that led to a Japanese victory at Pearl Harbor. From the war rooms of his giant battleship, *Yamato,* the largest ship in the world, Yamamoto and his officers planned another daring campaign. The admiral's attention focused on the tiny islands of Midway, west of Hawaii. Yamamoto believed that if he could capture this American position, the Japanese could use it as a base to launch an invasion of Hawaii. In addition, he guessed that the United States Navy would not allow Midway to fall without a fight. Yamamoto hoped to lure the rest of the American fleet out of Pearl Harbor into one decisive battle that would destroy America's sea power in the Pacific. This would give Japan an unassailable position. Yamamoto hoped that the United States would become convinced that it was too difficult to drive the Japanese out of all their island strongholds. Instead, Japan would be left alone to consolidate its empire while the United States focused its efforts on the war in Europe and the defeat of Nazi Germany.

After masterminding the Japanese attack on the American naval base at Pearl Harbor, Admiral Isoroku Yamamoto turned his attention to capturing the Midway Islands.

On May 5, 1942, Japanese Imperial General Headquarters issued Navy Order 18. It called for an attack on the western Aleutian Islands near Alaska and an invasion of Midway. The Japanese assault on the Aleutians was meant to divert some American ships away from the prime objective, Midway. The Americans would be forced to split their naval forces, making it easier for the Japanese to conquer them. On May 20, a directive went out to Japanese naval commanders from Admiral Yamamoto, describing the specific details of the upcoming campaign. Unknown to Yamamoto, his commanders were not the only ones who knew the specifics of the Midway operation.

At Pearl Harbor the U.S. Pacific fleet ran an organization known as the Combat Intelligence Unit. The unit was composed of experienced radio operators who listened in on Japanese military transmissions. These operators determined the approximate location of each ship that was sending or receiving messages and recorded the content of the messages.

Analyzing these messages was the responsibility of the cryptanalysts at the Intelligence Unit. The Japanese did not send their messages in plain language, but instead used a complicated code that included 45,000 five-digit groups of numbers. By analyzing enough of these coded messages, the analysts could begin to unlock the code and discover what each group of numbers meant. But it was time-consuming, painstaking work. To help them, the analysts had installed several IBM tabulators, the forerunners of computers. Coded messages were put on punch cards and fed into a tabulator that kept a record of them in its memory. Groups of numbers could then be compared to each other from different messages until the analysts began to figure out the meaning of each group.

The Combat Intelligence Unit was directed by Lieutenant Commander Joseph Rochefort, who had been put in charge of the operation in May 1941. Rochefort's analysts had been able to break down a large part of the Japanese naval code, JN25, and could read much of what was contained in the enemy's messages. In April 1942, for example, the analysts had figured out that the Japanese had decided to capture Port Moresby in New Guinea. Admiral Nimitz had sent part of his fleet into the area, and it engaged a Japanese aircraft carrier force in the Battle of the Coral Sea. The U.S. ships seriously damaged two of the Japanese carriers and put them out of action. As a result, the attack on Port Moresby was called off, and the Japanese carriers could not participate in the Battle of Midway.

Admiral Nimitz had, therefore, developed enormous confidence in the accuracy of the reports he received from Commander Rochefort and his group. In late May, the Combat Intelligence Unit received the encrypted message that Yamamoto had sent to all of his commanders about the upcoming invasion of Midway. Japanese code was supposed to be changed each month so the enemy could not begin to decipher it. However, the Japanese had postponed making any changes. Perhaps they had grown too confident with their success in the Pacific and believed that their code had not been broken. In any event, they were still using the same code in May as they had for April.

Yamamoto's message was analyzed and most of it was successfully deciphered in the Combat Intelligence Unit. However, the most important parts, such as the dates of the invasion and specific points, were very difficult to decipher because they had been encrypted in a more complicated code. Eventually, the analysts figured out that Midway was the target of the invasion. However, some of the top naval officials in Washington were still not convinced that the Japanese would allow their code to be broken. It might be a trick designed to confuse the Americans about the real goal of the Japanese attack. So Commander Rochefort set out to prove what he believed to be true. He had the American base at Midway send out a message to Pearl Harbor that their plant for distilling fresh water had broken. The Japanese intercepted this message and several days later they sent it out to all their naval units. The code used to identify Midway was identical to the one in Yamamoto's original message, proving

These World War II intelligence analysts worked with machines developed by American cryptographers to decode Japanese messages. The analysts were able to provide valuable information to the Pacific Fleet.

that these islands were indeed the target of the invasion.

Then the analysts worked on trying to discover when the invasion would occur. This information had also been encrypted in a complex code. But after many hours of work, it was finally cracked. Yamamoto's order had scheduled the attack on the Aleutian Islands for June 2, while the main assault would come on Midway the following day, June 3, 1942. Shortly after the American analysts had uncovered the enemy's plan of battle, the Japanese changed the code.

With this information, Admiral Nimitz began to develop his own battle strategy. Although he was greatly outnumbered by the Japanese fleet, his knowledge of where and when they were going to attack, and what ships would be involved, gave him at least a chance of achieving victory—a far better chance than if he had not known their plans. As Nimitz later wrote: "Midway was essentially a victory of intelligence. In attempting surprise, the Japanese were themselves surprised."

U.S. Commodore Matthew Perry was greeted at Edo Bay in Japan in an elaborate ceremony staged by the Japanese. Perry brought with him a request from President Millard Fillmore to open Japanese ports to foreign trade.

The Rising Sun

The events leading up to the war between Japan and the United States had begun almost a century earlier. In 1853, four American ships commanded by Commodore Matthew Perry arrived at Edo Bay in Japan. Perry's family had a long and very distinguished tradition of navy service. His older brother, Oliver Hazard Perry, had won a victory against the British on Lake Erie during the War of 1812. Matthew Perry had directed a successful amphibious landing at the Mexican port city of Vera Cruz in 1847 during the war between the United States and Mexico. Perry was also a strong advocate of developing steam ships to replace sailing vessels. Indeed, his flagship during the mission to Japan, the *Susquehanna*, was steam powered.

Perry arrived in Japan with a message from President Millard Fillmore, asking the Japanese to open their ports to trade and allow American ships to refuel there. By the 1850s, Japan had been closed to the West for almost 200 years. Portuguese and Dutch traders had arrived at Japanese ports during the 16th century, followed by Catholic missionaries who began converting some of the Japanese to Christianity. However the Japanese shogun, the military leader who ruled the country in the name of the emperor, was suspicious of the Christians. They seemed to believe in a God that was more powerful than the emperor, which might undermine imperial rule. Christians were persecuted in the 17th century by the Japanese government. In 1637, when they participated in a revolt against the government, thousands of Christians were slaughtered. Shortly afterward, the Japanese government closed the country to all westerners and missionaries, as well as traders. For the next 200 years, Japanese military power was strong enough to keep the westerners from penetrating the country. During the 19th century, however, the balance of power in the Far East changed. British gunboats had forced China, considered the strongest nation in the area, to open up various ports to Western trade in 1842. Japanese leaders watched these developments closely, realizing that their turn might be next.

Commodore Perry's approach had been reported before his ships were sighted at Edo. The Japanese created an elaborate ceremony to receive the Americans. They erected a beautiful silk pavilion on shore, where their leaders would meet the Americans. Perry, who knew the importance of ceremony to the Japanese, approached the pavilion accompanied by a long line of American sailors and marines as well as two marching bands that had sailed with him. "All this parade was but for effect," he later wrote. But that effect was important. He delivered his message and gave the Japanese time to consider it, indicating that he would return a few months later with an even larger force. The Japanese realized that they had no choice but to agree to the American terms.

Once Japan opened its doors to American traders, other countries followed. With a show of military power, Britain, France, and Russia also forced trading rights on Japan. The shogun lacked the power to stop the westerners. This so angered some powerful Japanese leaders that they overthrew the shogun. In 1868 they restored the leadership of the emperor, known as Meiji (enlightened rule). The new emperor also moved his capital from Kyoto to Edo, which was renamed Tokyo.

During the reign of Meiji, Japan began a rapid process of westernization. One of the most popular sayings of the period was "catch up, overtake." Western customs were spreading throughout the world, spearheaded by powerful European armies and navies that were carving huge empires. The Japanese intended to beat the westerners at their own game. Throughout the rest of the 19th century, the Japanese embarked on a massive industrialization effort, which included building miles and miles of railroads to speed transportation across the country. Japan also made a huge investment in shipbuilding. Large shipping concerns and other manufacturing companies were encouraged to open and given financial support by the government. Meanwhile, Japanese leaders visited the West to study democratic forms of government. Eventually, Japan instituted a legislature, called the Diet, with one house consisting of nobles and the other of representatives elected by the Japanese people. But voting was restricted to a small number of males, and the Diet was given relatively little authority. The tradition of imperial rule was far too strong. Political control remained in the hands of the leaders who advised the emperor and formed the Japanese cabinet.

One of the most important changes during the Meiji period was a modernization of the Japanese armed forces. In 1873, a new law required universal military service for all Japanese males. Japan also created a modern navy, including large battleships made of iron and steel. A popular slogan among the Japanese of the day was "a rich nation, a strong army." As one historian wrote: "Nationalism was an ideal cause. It tapped nicely into the revived sense of national identity and crisis triggered by the return of the foreign threat." The power of the West had required the Japanese to take stock of themselves. They needed to change or risk being left behind by other nations. In response, the Japanese experienced a new surge of nationalism. Internally, they began to modernize and westernize their industries and military forces. With this expensive army and navy, Japan wanted to assert itself in the Far East and create a position of leadership among the other nations there. All Japanese people were expected to work together to achieve this goal, united in the name of their divine emperor, Meiji.

For Japan to become a "rich nation," it needed to expand. The islands of Japan are relatively poor in the natural resources necessary to power industrialization. To the east, however, lay the vast Chinese province of Manchuria with rich deposits of iron and coal. An ally of the Chinese empire, Korea, offered the Japanese a large potential market to sell its manufactured goods. As Japanese nationalism and military power grew, the Chinese government was becoming weaker. China was being pulled apart by civil wars and found itself incapable of standing up to Western powers that were carving out their own areas of trade and influence on the Chinese mainland. China appeared to be a large power vacuum, and during the 1890s the Japanese began to move into it.

In 1894, the king of Korea called on the Chinese emperor to help him put down a revolt. The Japanese were outraged. Since the 1870s, Japan had used its own military power to create a sphere of influence in Korea and force the weak government to grant special trading rights to Japanese merchants. As soon as Chinese troops began marching into Korea, the Japanese sent in their own forces. The Japanese navy proved more than a match for the Chinese fleet, which lost several battles and was finally destroyed in 1895. Japanese forces took control of Korea and marched north into Manchuria. Finally, the Chinese agreed to a peace treaty that recognized that Korea was completely independent of China's influence and gave Japan the island of Taiwan, as well as the Liaotung Peninsula in Manchuria.

The emerging power of Japan represented a threat to Russia, which also wanted to extend its empire into Manchuria and Korea. With the help of Germany and France, the Russians forced Japan to give up the Liaotung Peninsula. Japan was not yet strong enough to argue, but Japanese leaders did not forget this humiliation. Several years later, the Russians persuaded China to allow them to use Liaotung to build a vast railroad from Moscow to Vladivostok, a Russian city on the Pacific Ocean. The Japanese were furious. Although the Russians said they would leave Manchuria, they remained, and tensions between Russia and Japan increased. The two countries were heading for war. In early 1904, both the Russians and the Japanese invaded Korea. Meanwhile, Japan attacked Russian naval vessels at Port Arthur in Manchuria. In two days the Japanese made a formal declaration of war.

Although the Russians were considered a great military power, they were no match for the Japanese. Over the next year and a half, the Japanese drove the Russians out of

Japan attacked Russian ships at Port Arthur in Manchuria. The two countries fought in 1905 over land in Korea and Manchuria.

Korea and captured Port Arthur. In May 1905, Japanese ships destroyed a large Russian fleet at the Battle of Tsushima Straits. The mighty Russian empire had been defeated but at a huge cost in money and lives to the Japanese. Both sides agreed to a peace treaty. The Japanese received the area of influence they wanted in Manchuria and Korea, and would take complete control of Korea a few years later. It was the first time a Western power, Russia, had ever been defeated by an Asian nation. Japanese nationalism and love for the emperor Meiji reached new heights.

Battle of Tsushima Straits

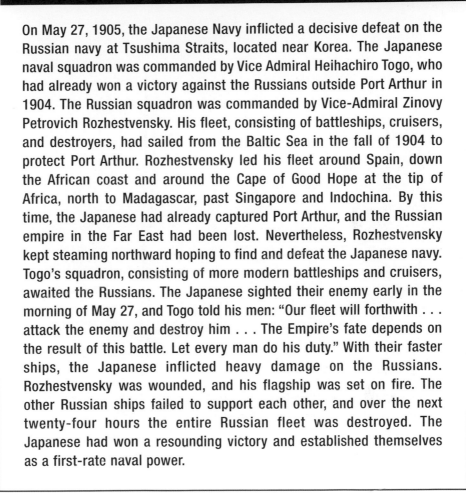

On May 27, 1905, the Japanese Navy inflicted a decisive defeat on the Russian navy at Tsushima Straits, located near Korea. The Japanese naval squadron was commanded by Vice Admiral Heihachiro Togo, who had already won a victory against the Russians outside Port Arthur in 1904. The Russian squadron was commanded by Vice-Admiral Zinovy Petrovich Rozhestvensky. His fleet, consisting of battleships, cruisers, and destroyers, had sailed from the Baltic Sea in the fall of 1904 to protect Port Arthur. Rozhestvensky led his fleet around Spain, down the African coast and around the Cape of Good Hope at the tip of Africa, north to Madagascar, past Singapore and Indochina. By this time, the Japanese had already captured Port Arthur, and the Russian empire in the Far East had been lost. Nevertheless, Rozhestvensky kept steaming northward hoping to find and defeat the Japanese navy. Togo's squadron, consisting of more modern battleships and cruisers, awaited the Russians. The Japanese sighted their enemy early in the morning of May 27, and Togo told his men: "Our fleet will forthwith . . . attack the enemy and destroy him . . . The Empire's fate depends on the result of this battle. Let every man do his duty." With their faster ships, the Japanese inflicted heavy damage on the Russians. Rozhestvensky was wounded, and his flagship was set on fire. The other Russian ships failed to support each other, and over the next twenty-four hours the entire Russian fleet was destroyed. The Japanese had won a resounding victory and established themselves as a first-rate naval power.

As one soldier who had participated in the Russo-Japanese War recalled: "I saw an awesome display of the Emperor's august and virtuous power as it spread afar. I positively leapt for joy when I saw the Rising Sun flag flying from the enemy strongholds . . . and realized how the blood in my veins too was Japanese blood."

A few years later, while Europe was engaged in

fighting World War I, the Japanese army marched into China. Japan took control of an area in Shandong Province in northeastern China near Manchuria. Japan also tried to force the weak Chinese government to let Japanese officials participate in running the country. While the Chinese agreed to a greater Japanese presence, they refused to let Japan play any role in the government. The Western Allies—including the United States—were concerned about the rising power of Japan. Following World War I, they agreed with Japan to limit each other's naval strength. At a conference held in Washington, D.C., in 1921, Great Britain, the United States, and Japan— among the world's leading naval powers—worked out an arrangement designed to prevent an arms race that might eventually lead to war. Britain and the United States each agreed to retain only a single naval base in the Pacific— the British held Singapore, and the United States retained Pearl Harbor. The three powers also agreed to limit the numbers of their large ships to a specific ratio. For every five U.S. ships and five British ships, Japan—a much smaller country—would be permitted three. Japanese military leaders, however, wanted to build even more. Nevertheless, a balance of power would be established in the Pacific that might keep peace in the area. Japan had also been recognized by the United States and Great Britain as an important nation.

The 1920s were a period of change in Japan. In 1927, a new emperor named Hirohito became the ruler. His reign was known as "Showa," which meant "Illustrious Peace." Meanwhile, the Japanese economy had slowed down, hurting many small farmers and merchants. The economic downturn, however, did not seem to have as much impact on the well-to-do owners of Japan's large manufacturing firms. They were accused of influencing the politicians to continue subsidizing the large firms.

Many Japanese criticized Western-style democracy for producing these corrupt politicians and longed for the return of strong military leaders, like the shoguns. In the early 1930s, Japan was hard hit by the Great Depression that swept across the United States and Europe. The Japanese looked eastward to the Asian mainland and began to think that if they controlled these areas, it might help to revitalize their economy.

On September 18, 1931, explosions occurred on the South Manchurian Railroad, which was owned by Japan. They were set off by Japanese soldiers who then blamed the incident on the Chinese. Japanese troops took over nearby Mukden, the capital of Manchuria, and a year later declared it an independent country under the influence of Japan. While some influential leaders in Japan opposed the military takeover, they were silenced by assassination. The Japanese prime minister was assassinated in 1932 for trying to reduce the power of the military. Following his death, all the prime ministers in the 1930s were from the military, which now firmly controlled the country.

Japan invested heavily in the mines and factories of Manchuria, which flourished economically. But the Japanese military wanted a much larger prize: China. The Chinese emperor had been deposed in 1911 by revolutionary leader Dr. Sun Yat-sen. When Dr. Sun died in 1925, he was succeeded by General Chiang Kai-shek. China was still wracked by civil war, as Chiang Kai-shek tried to deal with powerful Chinese warlords as well as the communist army led by Mao Zedong. The Japanese believed that this unsettled situation gave them the opportunity to intervene and take control of the entire country.

On July 7, 1937, a skirmish broke out between Chinese and Japanese soldiers at the Marco Polo Bridge near Peking. Japanese soldiers were permitted to be in the area and said that the Chinese had started the shooting.

Japanese soldiers destroyed the Chinese city of Nanking in December 1937. The Rape of Nanking, as it is called, included the massacre of thousands of Chinese civilians.

Whether or not it really happened that way, it was enough to provoke a Japanese invasion of China. In a few months, the Japanese controlled Peking and Shanghai. By December 1937, the Japanese had captured the capital city of Nanking. There Japanese troops unleashed a terrible massacre, called the Rape of Nanking, which claimed the lives of thousands and thousands of innocent Chinese civilians. In 1938 the Japanese captured Canton in the south of China, and by the following year every important city in the country was under their control. However, the Chinese did not give up. Chiang Kai-shek retreated westward into the Chinese heartland and kept fighting.

While the Japanese were engaged in China, Western

Europe was slowly drifting toward war. Japan had allied itself with the Axis powers—Nazi Germany and Fascist Italy. As Germany invaded Poland in September 1939, igniting World War II, Japan stood poised to expand its empire in the Pacific. Japanese empire building was inspired by a variety of motives. Many believed that Japan, under the leadership of the emperor, had been chosen to liberate Asia from Western influences and the power of China. The Japanese revered the emperor as a god and believed there could be no greater honor than to "the sacrifice of the life of a subject for the Emperor." But there were other motives for expansion, as well. Japanese leaders saw the Asian mainland as a fertile area for Japan's growing population, which seemed to be outgrowing the land available in Japan. In addition, Asia provided valuable natural resources that Japan desperately needed to power its industries and war machine.

By 1941, Japan was preparing for a larger war against the Western powers that still controlled colonies in the Far East. The Japanese wanted to move into British Malaya, a rich source of rubber; capture the British base at Singapore; and invade the Dutch East Indies where there were large deposits of oil. The Japanese hoped to become economically self-sufficient.

While the European powers were tied down with the war in Europe, Japan faced one major threat to its plans for expansion: the United States.

The United States
in the Pacific

The U.S. battleship *Maine* was blown up in the harbor of Havana, Cuba. The incident led to the Spanish-American War in 1898.

The United States became a major power in the Pacific during the Spanish-American War. In April 1898, Spain and the United States went to war over the Caribbean island of Cuba, where an independence movement was underway to throw off Spanish rule. The United States intervened on the side of the Cuban insurgents, after the U.S. battleship *Maine* was blown up in the harbor of Havana. Spain was blamed for the incident by the American press. Meanwhile the U.S. Asiatic Squadron under the command of Commodore George Dewey was ordered to steam into Manila Harbor in the Philippines—a colony of Spain—and prevent the Spanish fleet there from sailing toward Cuba.

On May 1, 1898, Commodore Dewey entered Manila harbor and opened fire on a much weaker Spanish fleet. In a few hours the entire Spanish squadron was destroyed. Dewey's forces eventually captured the city of Manila, ending Spanish control of the Philippines. As a result of the peace treaty signed by the United States and Spain, American forces took over the Philippines as well as Guam in the Pacific and Puerto Rico in the Caribbean. (Cuba was given its independence.) Suddenly, the United States had become a colonial power.

The rise of the United States on the world stage was part of America's Manifest Destiny. This phrase had been coined in the 1840s by the journalist John L. O'Sullivan, editor of *The United States Magazine and Democratic Review.* O'Sullivan and others like him believed that it was the country's destiny to spread its values and culture over the entire continent of North America. This explained the westward movement and justified a war with Mexico to take over California and the Southwest. Manifest Destiny would be used to justify a brutal warfare against Native American tribes, driving them off their hunting grounds to make room for white settlers. Finally, after American settlers had reached the Pacific coast, there seemed to be no reason for them to stop. Expansion should continue westward across the Pacific Ocean.

In fact, during the last part of the 18th century, American merchant ships had already begun pushing across the Pacific Ocean to China. They carried on a brisk trade in Chinese porcelain, silks, and tea, which were sold in the United States. In 1844, the United States and China signed the Treaty of Wanghia, formally granting Americans trading rights at various ports. The treaty also gave permission to American missionaries to build hospitals and churches in China. Protestant missionaries had been working on the mainland for several years, spreading

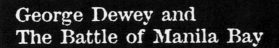

George Dewey and The Battle of Manila Bay

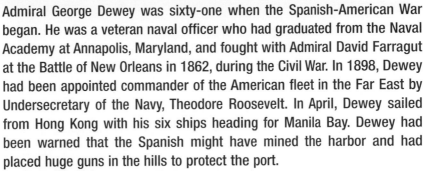

Admiral George Dewey was sixty-one when the Spanish-American War began. He was a veteran naval officer who had graduated from the Naval Academy at Annapolis, Maryland, and fought with Admiral David Farragut at the Battle of New Orleans in 1862, during the Civil War. In 1898, Dewey had been appointed commander of the American fleet in the Far East by Undersecretary of the Navy, Theodore Roosevelt. In April, Dewey sailed from Hong Kong with his six ships heading for Manila Bay. Dewey had been warned that the Spanish might have mined the harbor and had placed huge guns in the hills to protect the port.

Nevertheless, on the morning of May 1, Dewey entered the harbor, where the Spanish ships under the command of Admiral Patricio Montojo were under repair. As he spotted the enemy ships, Dewey gave the order to the captain of the U.S.S. *Olympia,* "You may fire when ready, Gridley." The American ships immediately began bombarding the seven Spanish ships in the harbor, and soon all of them had been set on fire. In the United States, Dewey was acclaimed a great hero for his victory. As a poem written by Eugene F. Ware put it: "O Dewey was the morning/Upon the first of May/And Dewey was the Admiral/Down in Manila Bay . . . " Dewey came back to the United States in 1899, where he was given a home by grateful New Yorkers and a sword by Congress.

Christianity among the Chinese people. The missionary work would continue for many decades, creating a powerful link between the United States and China.

At the same time, America had also been developing strong ties with the independent kingdom of Hawaii. During the 19th century, New England whaling ships regularly stopped at the port of Honolulu on the Hawaiian island of Oahu, which became a busy trading center for American products. American entrepreneurs also developed vast sugar plantations on the islands. The United States recognized the importance of the Hawaiian islands and soon after the victory in the Philippines, Congress annexed Hawaii and made it part of the emerging American empire. Hawaii was seen as an important naval base to help defend the Philippines, especially in the face of the growing empire of Japan, which had already defeated China during the Sino-Japanese War.

The rise of Japan and the United States as world powers was part of late 19th-century imperialism. European nations such as England, France, and Germany were establishing new colonies in Africa and the Far East. These colonies were rich sources of raw materials, like oil, rubber, and ivory. In addition they offered new markets for European manufactured goods. Many Europeans also believed that they had an obligation to bring the benefits of Western culture and Christianity to the rest of the world. They called it fulfilling the "white man's burden." In the United States, Captain A.T. Mahan wrote an influential book called *The Influence of Sea Power upon History, 1660-1783.* Published in 1890, this book called on the United States to develop a great navy. Mahan pointed out that countries could only achieve international greatness if they controlled the seas. "Whether they will or no," Mahan wrote, "Americans must now begin to look outward."

The United States felt a special responsibility for China because American missionaries and merchants had worked there for so long. In 1899, American Secretary of State John Hay proclaimed an Open Door policy for China. While Hay recognized that other nations, such as Great Britain, Germany, and Japan, had carved out spheres of influence in China, he called on them to safeguard Chinese indepen-dence and not to try to take control of the country. This policy would also ensure that American trade and influence in China continued. Several years later the United States tried to strengthen the Open Door policy and apply it specifically to Manchuria. However, Japan was already expanding its

This United States Navy cruiser was part of the "Great White Fleet" sent around the world by President Theodore Roosevelt to show America's power.

power in that area and refused to be bound by any policy that would reduce its influence. Already Japanese and U.S. interests were beginning to come into conflict.

In the meantime, the United States was building up a powerful fleet to back up its foreign policies. Influenced by the writings of Mahan, President Theodore Roosevelt embarked on a naval expansion program that made the United States Navy one of the world's largest. Between 1907 and 1909, Roosevelt sent the "Great White Fleet" on a cruise around the world to show off American power. The American navy continued to expand over the next few years, growing from 11 battleships in 1898 to 36 in 1913.

The following year, World War I broke out and American foreign policy focused primarily on Europe. At first, President Woodrow Wilson hoped to keep the United States out of the war. By 1917, however, Wilson realized that American troops must join the armies of Great Britain and France to defeat Germany. With victory finally won in 1918, Wilson wanted to craft a peace treaty based upon his Fourteen Points. Among other things, the Fourteen Points called for an end to colonial empires. Unfortunately, the victorious Allies did not agree with this principle. Japan, for example, which had joined the Allies during the war, held on to territory it had acquired from Germany on the Chinese mainland. Wilson also hoped to prevent future wars by persuading the world's countries to join a League of Nations to work together to keep the peace. However, a majority of the U.S. Congress feared that such a world organization would try to dictate American foreign policy and refused to join it.

Instead, the United States began to retreat from the world stage. As historians Allan Millett and Peter Maslowski have written, American foreign policy "shrank to three goals: defending the continental United States and its overseas possessions from foreign attack," "keeping European powers out of the Western Hemisphere," "and preserving China's sovereignty and territorial integrity." The United States also tried to prevent future wars through naval treaties with Great Britain and Japan to limit the size of their fleets. As a result of this treaty, signed in 1922, the United States was forced to destroy 15 new large ships, which together had cost more than $300 million to build. However, the treaty allowed the United States to retain 18 battleships—almost twice as many as Japan—and convert 2 battle cruisers into aircraft carriers.

In China, the United States continued to support the Open Door policy. But there was little desire on the part of the American people to back up the policy with force. After the devastation of World War I, Americans retreated to a policy of isolation. Most people hoped that their country would be protected from invasion by two large oceans and would never need to become involved in another war. While some of America's political leaders recognized that Japan might pose a threat to peace in Asia, they were content to let the navy rely on its existing battleships, destroyers, and gunboats to protect America's position in the Far East. In addition, the United States maintained only a single naval base at Pearl Harbor, which had been specified by the naval treaty. This meant that it would be difficult to defend the Philippines in case of attack because the base at Pearl Harbor was so far to the east. U.S. ships would have no place to refuel if they were called on to fight a war in the western Pacific.

The Great Depression of 1929 cut even further into expenditures for the navy. As a result of the economic crash, very little money was available for ship building. In 1932, President Herbert Hoover stated that although "he would fight for Continental United States, he would not fight for Asia." This statement came at the same time that Japan was expanding its power in Manchuria. Hoover also refused to impose economic sanctions (cut off trade) with Japan out of fear that this might lead to war with the Japanese.

In 1933, Franklin D. Roosevelt became president of the United States. Roosevelt's domestic program, called the New Deal, was aimed at improving the economy and putting millions of unemployed Americans back to work. The New Deal included funding for vast public works projects to build roads, bridges, and naval ships. Roosevelt had a keen interest in the navy, having served as assistant naval secretary during Wilson's administration. The president earmarked $238 million to build 32 ships over the next three years, including carriers, cruisers, and destroyers. Additional funds were authorized to strengthen the navy during the rest of the decade. However, U.S. naval strength still fell behind Japan's forces. By 1939, the Japanese navy had more carriers, cruisers, destroyers, and submarines than the United States. The Japanese government had decided not to abide by the naval treaty of 1922, thereby greatly expanding the strength of its navy.

Meanwhile, the Japanese were increasing their grip on China. American missionaries were being driven out of the country, as the Japanese indiscriminately bombed homes, churches, and hospitals. However, most of the American people still believed in a policy of isolation. According to a poll taken in 1938, 70 percent of all Americans said that we should totally withdraw from China.

A year later, Europe was plunged into war as Nazi Germany invaded Poland. At first, the United States hoped to stay out of the conflict as it had done during the first years of World War I. According to a series of neutrality acts, passed during the 1930s, America was prevented from loaning money or selling any arms to nations involved in war. By 1940, however, Nazi armies had conquered all of Western Europe, except Great Britain. President Roosevelt and many Congressional leaders realized that the United States could not stay on the sidelines indefinitely. In 1940, Congress approved legislation doubling the size of the combat navy. Meanwhile, the U.S. naval fleet moved its base to Pearl

This poster announcing "The New Germany" was issued in 1933, the same year that Adolf Hitler became chancellor. A World War I soldier and a storm trooper flank the podium.

Harbor, a signal to the Japanese that they must stop their powerful armies from overrunning much of China. The president had already warned that if conquest was not stopped "let no one imagine that America will escape, that America may expect mercy, that this Western

Hemisphere will not be attacked."

In early 1941, under the terms of the Lend-Lease Act, the United States broke its neutrality and agreed to "sell, transfer, exchange, lease, lend" any war material "to the government of any country whose defense the President deems vital to the defense of the United States." This meant specifically Great Britain, which was fighting against the Nazis.

Later in 1941, Japan conquered French Indochina. There was little France could do since it was already part of the Nazi empire, which had an alliance with Japan. Roosevelt responded immediately by taking control of all Japanese financial assets in U.S. banks. The United States also stopped all exports to Japan. The most important of these exports was oil, which the Japanese desperately needed to run their ships, tanks, and other armored vehicles. Great Britain also cut off all exports to Japan, including oil and rubber. By September 1941, Japanese leaders had decided to start a war with the United States unless the embargo on imports could be ended. However, the U.S. Secretary of State Cordell Hull said the embargo would only be lifted if Japan would begin withdrawing from China and Indochina immediately.

The new Japanese Prime Minister General Hideki Tojo had at first favored negotiations with the United States, but he refused to accept Hull's position. The Japanese, meanwhile were planning the attack on Pearl Harbor. They hoped that a single knockout blow against the U.S. fleet would convince America to agree to peace. The United States and Japan were now at an impasse. Neither side was prepared to back down. On December 7, 1941, while Japanese diplomats were still negotiating in Washington, Japan attacked Pearl Harbor. Over 2,400 Americans were dead and almost

The Japanese ambassador to the United States, Admiral Nomura (left), and special envoy Saburo Kuruso (right) are shown leaving a meeting with the U.S. secretary of state moments after the Japanese attack on Pearl Harbor.

1,200 were wounded. President Roosevelt called it "a day that shall live in infamy." He vowed that "no matter how long it may take us to overcome this premeditated invasion, the American people in their righteous might will win through to absolute victory."

Hideki Tojo had a long and successful military career before being appointed prime minister of Japan.

Japan's Early Successes

Soon after Japan's victory at Pearl Harbor, Admiral Yamamoto wrote a letter to his sister. "Well, war has begun at last," he said. "But in spite of all the clamor that is going on, we could lose it. I can only do my best." Yamamoto believed that the Japanese had about six months to achieve a series of lightning victories in the Pacific before the United States would recover its balance. If the Japanese acted quickly, they might create an empire so large and powerful that the United States might give up the war and negotiate a peace treaty.

Japanese war leaders intended to move swiftly south against the British colonies of Hong Kong and Malaya, the Dutch East Indies, and the American commonwealth of the Philippines.

This plan had the strong support of the Japanese Prime Minister Hideki Tojo. A veteran of the armed forces, Tojo had graduated from a military academy in 1905 and soon afterward joined the occupation army in Manchuria. He was gradually promoted for his exemplary service in a variety of military posts and in the 1930s became head of the Manchurian military police, a powerful position in the government. During the Sino-Japanese War, Tojo led an army that took control of Inner Mongolia. In 1938 he became vice minister of war in the Japanese cabinet, war minister two years later, and finally prime minister.

No sooner had the Japanese attacked Pearl Harbor, than their planes swooped down on the Philippines. Although the Philippine Islands were still part of the United States, the islands were self-governing and expected to be given their complete independence during the 1940s. The armed forces, however, were commanded by General Douglas MacArthur. General MacArthur had assembled an army of over 100,000 men, many of them Filipino militiamen with little training. MacArthur had expected that his air force of fighters and bombers would provide a strong defensive shield to protect the Philippines. But on December 7, 1941, while his planes were parked on the runways of Clark and Iba airfields near Manila, they were struck by the Japanese. Many planes and their pilots and ground crews were lost in the attack. The Japanese were now ready to begin their invasion of the Philippines.

At the same time, units of the Japanese 23rd army stationed in China invaded the British colony of Hong Kong. This was a major trading center in the Far East. Hong Kong did not have very strong defenses, and the Japanese were able to mount a successful siege. They took control of Hong Kong on December 25, 1941. The cruelty of the Japanese on mainland China in such incidents as the Rape of Nanking was now repeated in Hong Kong. "When Hong Kong was captured," one historian wrote, "Japanese troops entered St. Stephen's College, then used as a military hospital, bayoneted approximately seventy prisoners, tortured and mutilated others, and raped the Chinese nurses."

Japanese forces were also beginning their invasion of another British colony, Malaya. Leading Japan's 25th army was General Tomoyuki Yamashita, who proposed to make a series of landings at various points along the Malay Peninsula. Although Yamashita had fewer troops than the British, he had more planes. These planes became a decisive advantage for Japan. To stop the invasion, the British had sent out a naval task force spearheaded by the battleship *Prince of Wales* and the heavy cruiser *Repulse*. On December 10, 1941, Japanese planes sent out from Saigon in Vietnam spotted the two large ships. Immediately they swept in, hitting the *Prince of Wales* with a torpedo that disabled its steering and sent it listlessly steaming around in a circle. The *Prince of Wales* was hit again and again, while Japanese planes had also been sending torpedoes into the *Repulse*. Both ships sank, giving Japan control of the sea around Malaya. Thus the first two weeks of the war had seen nothing but Japanese victories.

In the Philippines, the Japanese success continued. At first General MacArthur hoped to defend the capital of Manila on the island of Luzon. On December 22, Japan's army led by General Masaharu Homma invaded Luzon north of Manila at Lingayen Gulf. When American forces under the command of General Jonathan Wainwright proved unable to stop the Japanese, MacArthur ordered a retreat to the peninsula of Bataan. This was an area covered with heavy jungle, where MacArthur hoped he could hold out against a

The British heavy cruiser *Repulse* sank off the coast of the Malay Peninsula after being torpedoed by Japanese aircraft.

Japanese army that numbered almost 200,000. Just south of Bataan, MacArthur had also fortified the island of Corregidor. On December 29, the Japanese began a massive assault against MacArthur's position.

At first General Homma was stunned to discover that the assault was not successful, even with Japanese superiority in the air. By the end of January, the Japanese had received more troops and were ready to renew their attacks. President Franklin Roosevelt realized that MacArthur was essential to any American efforts to stop the advances of the Japanese later in the war. Recognizing that Bataan could not be defended much longer, the president ordered that MacArthur be evacuated from the Philippines and sent to Australia. On March 11, 1942, MacArthur was spirited off Bataan in a motor torpedo boat. Fortunately, he was able to elude the Japanese naval blockade although at one point his boat was almost spotted by a Japanese battleship. Bataan surrendered on April 9. The captured American and Filipino soldiers were led away on what became known as the notorious Bataan Death March. Between 600 and 700 Americans and as many as 7,000 Filipinos died at the hands of their Japanese captors. General Wainwright continued the defense of the Philippines from Corregidor, but he was finally forced to surrender on May 6, 1942.

While the Japanese were advancing in the Philippines, other islands were also falling to Japanese armies. The British colony on the island of Borneo had been invaded in mid-December. A month later, Japan's armies had taken full control of the colony and driven out the weak army of British defenders. Borneo provided Japan with large oil supplies to run its war machine. Prime Minister Tojo told the Japanese Diet that the armies had 70 oil wells fully operational on the island. "The oil problem of Japan was solved . . . The Japanese could expect to get 500,000 barrels of oil from these fields in the next year."

East of Borneo lay the Malay Peninsula, one of the crown jewels in the British empire. Malaya was rich in tin mines as well as rubber, grown on scores of plantations located throughout the dense jungle that covered the peninsula. To protect their treasured colony, the British had built a great fortress city at Singapore, located on an island at the southern tip of the Malayan Peninsula. Huge guns bristled around the city to defend it from

The Japanese forced American and Filipino prisoners of war to carry their wounded and sick soldiers on the Bataan Death March.

invasion. They had been placed in positions built of rein-forced concrete and faced permanently seaward, because the British were convinced that any invasion would come from the sea. No army, they believed, could march through the jungles of the peninsula and attack Singapore from the land side. The Japanese would prove that the British had made a terrible miscalculation.

General Yamashita's forces began advancing down both sides of the Malay Peninsula in December 1941. Although the British tried to establish defensive positions and halt the advances, each time the Japanese outwitted them. They would send their tanks against the British defenses, while groups of infantry worked their way around the flanks and attacked the defenders from the rear. Meanwhile, Japanese aircraft controlled the skies, making defense for the British even more difficult. In Malaya, the Japanese proved themselves to be the masters of jungle warfare, while the British who had run the colony for a century had never learned how to fight in the jungles.

The Japanese traveled light, carrying a minimum of food and equipment. The British, on the other hand, in the words of one officer, were "equipped like Christmas trees with heavy boots, . . . packs, haversacks, water bottles . . . and even greatcoats . . . so they could hardly walk, much less fight." The Japanese infantry often relied on bicycles to move forward or outflank the enemy. Sometimes the rubber tires would burst because of the heat, so the Japanese would keep riding their bicycles on the rims. Little by little they pushed the British back down the island. "The key difference," as one historian wrote, "was in morale: the British were falling back and they knew it, the Japanese were advancing at a great rate and they knew that, too." No sooner would the British try to establish a new line of defense, than the Japanese would find a way to outflank it by cutting their way through the jungles or finding small rivers in the rear and using boats to advance along them. Japan's bomber squadrons were also carrying out more frequent raids on Singapore itself. Nevertheless, the British seemed convinced that somehow the Japanese would finally be stopped before they reached the island fortress. Throughout December and early January, British citizens living at Singapore continued to stage holiday dances, arrange tennis matches, and play cricket as if no war were occurring. By mid-January, however, the important city of Kuala Lumpur had fallen and by the end of the month, all British troops had retreated onto the island for the last ditch defense of Singapore. Meanwhile, women and children were being evacuated by boat.

The British armies had retreated 450 miles in 53 days. The entire Malay Peninsula had been lost and only Singapore, itself, remained. Then the Japanese began their amphibious assault on the island. According to one eyewitness, "Singapore was crying out for leadership." British morale was extremely low, and their commander, General Arthur Percival, seemed incapable of stopping the Japanese. For the next two weeks, General Yamashita's troops pushed across the island until they stood only a few thousand yards from Singapore's last defenses. The guns of the great fortress, which might have helped stop the attacks, were unfortunately pointed the wrong way and could offer little help. The British were running short of water, and the civilians still remaining in Singapore seemed to have little desire to continue the battle. Percival had also convinced himself that the Japanese outnumbered him and had the resources to overrun Singapore. Yamashita, however, knew better. After leaving many troops to control the Malay Peninsula, his army in Singapore was greatly outnumbered by the British. As he wrote in his diary: "My attack on Singapore was a bluff—a bluff that worked. I had 30,000 men and was outnumbered more than three to one. I knew that if I had to fight long for Singapore, I would be beaten. That is why the surrender had to be at once. I was very frightened all the time that the British would discover our numerical weakness and lack of supplies and force me into disastrous street fighting."

Percival had no such intention. Instead, he surrendered on February 15, 1942, after receiving assurances from Yamashita

The Japanese battleship *Huso* is followed by the *Kirisima* and a squadron of ships during maneuvers off the coast of Malaya.

that the British would be protected. Unfortunately, the Japanese did not live up to their promises. According to one historian, "The troops surged into the Alexandra Hospital [in Singapore], bayoneted every person they saw, entered the operating room, where an operation was going on, and bayoneted the patient, the anesthetist, and the surgeon. From there they moved through the hospital and killed every person they found." The fall of Singapore freed Japanese troops to assist their comrades in the battle for Burma. By the end of April, the British had been defeated there and pushed back into India.

While the Japanese were taking control of Malaya and Burma, they were also attacking the Dutch East Indies. These included the islands of Sumatra, Java, the Celebes, eastern Borneo, and the Moluccas. On January 23, 1942, a Japanese task force carried an invasion force toward the oil port of Balikpapan in eastern Borneo. The Japanese were intercepted by a small American naval squadron that sank several troops ships, then retreated. However, the Japanese invasion of Borneo continued. By early February, they occupied the east coast of the island as well as the nearby Celebes.

Japanese control of the air as well as superior naval power gave them a tremendous advantage. In mid-February a small Allied squadron under the command of Dutch Admiral Karel Doorman tried to prevent the Japanese from capturing the oil port of Palembang in Sumatra. But the Allied air force was no match for the Japanese. Approximately two weeks later, February 27, 1942, Admiral Doorman's ships engaged the Japanese again as they were attempting to invade Java. Greatly outnumbered, Doorman lost two cruisers and three destroyers during the Battle of the Java Sea. The battle continued on the next night as Doorman sunk several Japanese transports carrying troops for the invasion. But more of his ships were destroyed and eventually his entire squadron was knocked out of action. On March 6, 1942, Batavia, the capital of the Dutch East Indies fell to Japan. Almost 100,000 troops were captured. Once again, Japanese soldiers were guilty of terrible atrocities—raping and murdering innocent civilians.

By the spring of 1942, Japan was completely victorious in the Pacific. Prime Minister Tojo had told the Japanese people that they would "construct a glorious tomorrow" as "builders of Greater East Asia." The newly conquered territories were incorporated into the Greater East Asia

Co-Prosperity Sphere. The island strongholds would provide not only raw materials, but also a string of outer defenses for the Japanese homelands. In some parts of the Pacific, the Japanese were at first received as liberators. Nogi Haramuchi was attached to Japan's navy and sent to Celebes as part of the occupying force. As he wrote: "In 1942 I thought occupying a country was a wonderful thing. When our ship arrived at the Celebes . . . I saw wide stretches of uncultivated soil. 'We can develop this land and introduce Japanese technology here,' I thought . . . We traveled through the southern part of the Celebes by car. All seemed to be functioning well, and we Japanese were being treated as liberators who had expelled the Dutch for the [people]. The haughty Dutch who had lorded it over the Indies found themselves prisoners overnight."

While the Japanese were occupying the Pacific islands, the American Pacific fleet was attempting to harass Japan's navy. Nothing more was possible for the American fleet, which had been badly damaged at Pearl Harbor. However, the American aircraft carriers were still in operation because they had not been in Hawaii during the attack. U.S. planes based on these carriers raided Japanese bases during February and March. Then, in April, the United States staged a daring attack on the Japanese mainland. On April 18, sixteen B-25 bombers under the command of Lieutenant Colonel James H. Doolittle took off from the carrier USS *Hornet*. The planes flew over Japan, dropping their bombs on Tokyo as well as other cities. The distance from the carriers was too far for the planes to return, so they flew on toward China and crash landed or the crews bailed out and parachuted to safety. Although the raid did little damage, the Japanese were stunned that their cities could be attacked, and Japan's leaders were embarrassed. The raid, which was highly publicized in the United States,

Lieutenant Colonel James Doolittle inspected a bomb aboard the USS *Hornet* before the United States began its bombing of Tokyo.

also served as a great morale booster at a time when there was very little to lift the spirits of Americans.

Less than a month later, an American squadron under the command of Admiral Frank Jack Fletcher intercepted a Japanese invasion of Port Moresby in southern New Guinea. The Japanese wanted to occupy the port to give them an advanced base to bomb Australia. Fletcher's fleet included the carriers *Yorktown* and *Lexington*. On the morning of May 7, 1942, American planes sank the Japanese aircraft carrier *Shoho* during the Battle of the Coral Sea. The naval battle continued on the following day, as planes from both sides attacked each other's ships. American planes hit the Japanese carrier *Shokaku*, knocking her out of the battle. Japanese bombers struck the American carriers, damaging the *Yorktown* and sinking the *Lexington*. However, the Japanese decided to call off their invasion of Port Moresby.

Unknown to both sides, Japanese victories were coming to an end. Soon, the tide of battle would begin to turn.

Preparing
for Midway

The aircraft carrier USS *Yorktown* was being repaired in dry dock at Pearl Harbor. By May 30, the carrier was ready for the Battle of Midway.

When he heard about the American air attack on Japan, Admiral Isoroku Yamamoto was dismayed. To think that an enemy aircraft carrier could launch planes against the Japanese homeland! In Yamamoto's mind, it was an insult to the honor of Japan and the power of its military leaders. All the more reason that the American navy in the Pacific, especially its carriers, must be destroyed.

Yamamoto had in mind a plan that would accomplish this goal. It called for an attack on the American base at Midway, which lay about 1,100 miles west of Pearl Harbor. In the past, Midway had served as a refueling station for American ships. Currently, it was primarily used by the United States Navy to send out patrol planes into the Pacific.

A successful attack on Midway, Yamamoto reasoned, would give the Japanese navy a launching site for another assault on Pearl Harbor. But, even more importantly, he was almost sure that the Americans would try to defend Midway by sending out their Pacific fleet to confront the Japanese.

By the spring of 1942, Japan's sea power in the Pacific was overwhelming. Admiral Yamamoto had approximately 86 fighting ships compared to less than one-third that number for the United States. There were four heavy Japanese carriers and two light carriers, while the Americans had only three carriers. Japan had 11 battleships, 10 heavy cruisers, and 53 destroyers, while the United States had no battleships, only 6 heavy cruisers, and 17 destroyers. Yamamoto knew that the Japanese superiority would not continue too much longer. From his knowledge of the United States, he understood that its manufacturing capabilities were far greater than those of Japan. Once America began gearing up its war industries to produce ships, planes, and weapons, Japan would be defeated unless the United States could be forced out of the war with one grand assault. It was a gamble, and Yamamoto realized it, but he also believed that there was no other choice.

During May, the Japanese forces gathered at three different staging areas: in northern Japan at Ominato; in southern Japan at Hashirajima; and south on the Japanese held islands of Saipan and Guam. Yamamoto's plan called for a diversionary force to steam out of Ominato to attack the American islands of Attu and Kiska as well as the base at Dutch Harbor—all in the Aleutians. Two other large fleets would leave Hashirajima and descend on Midway from the northwest. One of these fleets was commanded by Admiral Chuichi Nagumo. He had been the victor at Pearl Harbor six months earlier and more recently had been operating in the Indian Ocean harassing the British colony of Ceylon (Sri Lanka). The second fleet was led by Admiral

Nobutake Kondo, who had been trying to find the carriers that had launched the Doolittle raid against Japan. Another fleet steamed westward from Guam and Saipan, carrying the Japanese army that would invade Midway as well as its support group of heavy cruisers.

Yamamoto's plan, which was known as the MI Operation, called for a rapid series of coordinated strikes. They would begin with the attack on the Aleutians, designed to divert attention from the main assault and perhaps siphon off some of the American ships. On the next day, Admiral Nagumo would start to attack Midway. Nagumo's First Carrier Task Force included the four Japanese heavy carriers: *Akagi, Kaga, Hiryu,* and *Soryu.* In addition to launching attack planes against Midway, Nagumo was also to be prepared to confront the American carriers that Yamamoto hoped would come out from Pearl Harbor to defend Midway. On the third day of the attack, the invasion would begin, supported by Admiral Kondo's task force. Meanwhile, Admiral Yamamoto, would remain behind the main naval contingents with a large fleet of battleships. These would be poised to strike the American navy, once the Japanese were certain where they were located. Yamamoto's force, together with the planes and ships of Admiral Nagumo, would then overwhelm the U.S. fleet and destroy it.

The Japanese plan was complicated. It depended on having accurate and rapid intelligence that would tell Yamamoto and his commanders the positions of the American carriers. Nagumo would also find himself in a somewhat difficult situation. At some point in the battle, he might need to decide whether to send his planes against the American carriers or against Midway itself. A wrong decision might leave his own carriers open to attack from American planes and decide the outcome of the entire engagement. On May 25, 1942, Admiral Yamamoto met with his senior officers for a festive celebration to toast the

Admiral Chuichi Nagumo was victorious at Pearl Harbor. Later he was chosen to command a larger Japanese fleet in the attack of Midway.

emperor and begin the campaign that everyone confidently believed would end in total victory. Two days later, the fleets began leaving their staging areas eastward toward Midway.

What Yamamoto did not know was that the American naval commander in chief at Pearl Harbor, Admiral Chester Nimitz, knew most of the particulars of the Japanese plan. As mentioned earlier, U.S. intelligence officers had broken Japan's naval code. But even with this knowledge, Nimitz was facing a great challenge. He faced a highly confident enemy that had just completed a string of impressive victories in the Pacific. What's more, they vastly outnumbered his own small fighting force. Nimitz sent out urgent messages to his two carrier task forces to rendezvous as fast as possible at Pearl Harbor. Admiral Frank Jack Fletcher steamed northward following the Battle of the Coral Sea. Although he had lost the carrier *Lexington,* he still had the *Yorktown.* However, this large carrier had been badly damaged during the battle and might not be repaired at Pearl Harbor soon enough to participate in the upcoming action at Midway. From the Solomon Islands, another task force under the command of Admiral William F. (Bull) Halsey also steamed northward. Among Halsey's ships were the carriers *Hornet* and *Enterprise.* The *Hornet* had launched Doolittle's raid on Japan.

While the ships were heading toward Pearl Harbor, Nimitz also began the job of fortifying Midway. The base included two small islands, Sand and Eastern. The task of defending them was the responsibility of Navy Commander Cyril T. Simard and Marine Lieutenant Colonel Harold Shannon. In early May, Nimitz met with these two officers and together they decided what the islands would need to put up a defense. Then Nimitz began directing a steady stream of supplies toward Midway. Under the leadership of Simard and Shannon, the marines began digging trenches and laying yards and yards of barbed wire. Antiaircraft guns were put in place and command posts were dug out underground so they could withstand a heavy bombardment by the Japanese.

Midway also received aerial reinforcements consisting of bombers and fighter planes. Bunkers were dug to protect the planes so they would not be left out on runways as the planes had been at Pearl Harbor and Clark Field in the Philippines, where they became sitting ducks for the Japanese. In addition, Midway had patrol planes that were sent out regularly to scout for the approaching Japanese fleet. Each day, they ranged 700 miles west from the base in an arc of 180 degrees. As one high ranking American officer put it: "The problem at Midway is one of hitting before we are hit."

Near the end of May, Halsey's Task Force 16 and Fletcher's Task Force 17 steamed into Pearl Harbor. Bull Halsey was one of the most colorful admirals in the United States Navy. An expert on carrier warfare, he was beloved by his men for his intrepid spirit and love of battle. He had been the perfect officer to launch the raid against Japan in April. Halsey yearned to be a part of the upcoming battle at Midway. But he had contracted a debilitating skin condition that caused him to itch constantly, and his doctors ordered him into the hospital at Pearl Harbor. As his replacement, Halsey and Nimitz selected Admiral Raymond Spruance. Thin and battle hardened, Spruance commanded the destroyer squadron of Task Force 16. Although he had little experience with carriers, Nimitz was convinced that Spruance was the right man for the job. "Spruance," he said, "was the type who took the war to the enemy. He was bold, but not to the point of being reckless. He had a certain caution and a feeling for battle."

Spruance planned that he and Admiral Fletcher's Task Force 17 should await the Japanese to the northeast of Midway. Spruance believed the naval intelligence that had uncovered the Japanese battle plan and knew approximately where to find their battle fleets. However, Spruance was still concerned that the Japanese plan might somehow change. Yamamoto might bypass Midway and head directly for Pearl Harbor. Therefore, instead of steaming west to meet the Japanese fleet, missing it, and allowing the enemy to get in behind him on the way to Pearl Harbor, Spruance decided to lie in wait east of Midway. Then he would be in the best position to strike the Japanese fleet, regardless of its destination.

While Spruance was finalizing his plans, repairs were underway on the carrier *Yorktown*. It had been damaged at the Coral Sea, and the workmen at Pearl Harbor were

Admiral Raymond Spruance was a bold and experienced naval officer by the time he led U.S. Task Force 16 into battle in the Pacific.

afraid it might take several weeks to repair the ship. "We must have this ship back in three days," Nimitz informed them. His latest intelligence told him that the Japanese strike was planned for early June, and he needed a third carrier to give him a chance of victory. Welders, electricians, and mechanics went to work at Pearl Harbor, clearing away the debris that had been created when the *Yorktown* had been hit by the Japanese. They worked around the clock making all the necessary repairs to the ship's hull. By May 30, the *Yorktown* was ready to be put back to sea, outfitted with additional planes for the coming battle.

The three carriers along with the planes stationed at

Midway would give the American forces a slight edge in air power over the Japanese. Yamamoto's carriers had approximately 325 aircraft, including bombers and fighter planes. The United States had almost 350 planes.

Once the *Yorktown* was ready to go, Admiral Fletcher left Pearl Harbor with his task force to join Spruance's task force at a point about 325 miles east of Midway at a position called Point Luck. As one young lieutenant wrote in his diary: "We have history in the palm of our hands during the next week or so. If we are able to keep our presence unknown to the enemy and surprise them with a vicious attack on their carriers, the United States Navy should once more be supreme in the Pacific."

Meanwhile, the Japanese were advancing with almost no idea of what the American forces were doing to defend against them. Part of Yamamoto's plan had been to deploy Japanese submarines and patrol seaplanes far in advance of the main fleet. Their mission was to watch for American ships leaving Pearl Harbor and track them so the Japanese would know their positions. However, the submarines were not outfitted with crews soon enough to carry out their mission as advanced scouts. Since some of the subs were also supposed to provide fuel to the seaplanes, they were also unable to do their job. As a result, Admiral Yamamoto had no clear intelligence of where the American carriers were located. Indeed, by the time the Japanese submarines finally did get into place between Midway and Hawaii on June 3, the American task forces had already left Pearl Harbor and were nearing the rendezvous at Point Luck. The Japanese subs had missed them.

Admiral Nagumo's task force was advancing eastward without knowing the location of the enemy. He didn't know that the submarines had failed in their mission. The Japanese had decided to maintain a radio silence so the Americans would not be able to determine the Imperial

Midway Islands

Location:	Central Pacific
	1150 miles northwest of Hawaii
	2250 miles east of Japan
Atoll:	Circular coral reefs with opening into a lagoon
Two Main Islands	
Larger:	Sand Island–eastern island
Smaller:	Eastern Island–western island
Size:	Two square miles
Background:	First American landings in 1859
	Annexed by the United States in 1867
	Cable station built on Sand Island in 1903
	Commercial airport opened in 1935

fleet's position. Therefore, Yamamoto was prevented from communicating with Nagumo.

On Midway, American marines were making final preparations for the coming attack. They were dug in along Midway behind strong defensive positions and had even received a small contingent of tanks to aid them in the battle. During the early days of June, patrol squadrons were continually sent westward looking for the enemy's navy that was supposed to be approaching. On June 2, a heavy fog made long-range patrolling impossible. But on the following day, the pilots were at it again. They took off at 4:15 in the morning to search for the Japanese. At 400 miles westward, the search planes had found nothing. But one patrol plane had pushed much farther—700 miles out from Midway. As the pilot looked down, he spotted a massive flotilla of Japanese ships on the horizon. Radio messages were immediately sent to Midway, describing the number of ships and their exact location.

The Battle of Midway was about to begin.

The Battle Begins

Crewmen aboard the USS *Enterprise* in the Pacific Ocean are shown unfolding the wings of torpedo bombers in preparation for a raid on Japanese forces.

Shortly after noontime, on June 3, 1942, American B-17 bombers taxied down the runway at Midway headed for what they thought might be the "main body" of the Japanese fleet. At least, this is what the reports stated from the U.S. patrol plane that had spotted the enemy. Captain Cyril Simard, commander at Midway, wasn't so sure. American intelligence, which had cracked the Japanese code, expected the enemy's carrier task force to be heading for Midway on a course farther northward. But Simard wasn't going to wait to find out. He believed in hitting the Japanese before they could launch their planes and strike Midway. So he gave the order to fly.

Under the command of Colonel Walter Sweeney, the bombers set off on a 600-mile journey to strike the Japanese fleet. It took most of the afternoon before they spotted the enemy ships. Sweeney's planes dodged Japanese antiaircraft fire and dropped their bombs, then headed back for Midway before running out of gasoline. But the Japanese were veterans of naval warfare, and their ships zigzagged to avoid being hit by the bombs falling from the B-17s. None of the enemy ships were damaged. The first round had gone to the Japanese.

By evening, American reconnaissance reports had confirmed that Sweeney's bombers had struck the Japanese invasion convoy, not the carrier task force. The intelligence officers, who had broken the Japanese code, had been right after all about the route that the enemy invasion force would take. They had also figured out something else: The date of the Japanese assault on the Aleutian Islands. On June 3, Japanese planes struck the American base at Dutch Harbor. Admiral Nimitz had sent a small task force to the Aleutians to deal with the invasion that he knew would follow. But Nimitz also realized that this was only a diversion. He kept most of his ships ready to deal with the main Japanese thrust that was aimed at Midway.

In the early morning hours of June 4, Admiral Nagumo was preparing to launch the Midway assault from his carrier task force. He had not been told about the bomber attack the previous day. Admiral Yamamoto had decided to maintain radio silence with Nagumo's fleet so the Americans would not discover his location. In fact, Yamamoto was still mystified by the fact that the enemy had somehow known where the invasion force could be found. So far, Admiral Frank Jack Fletcher on the *Yorktown* had not been as successful in pinpointing Nagumo's task force. But Fletcher knew that if American intelligence had been right about the Aleutian attack and

Japanese Zero fighter planes, such as the one shown here, were used at Midway to provide cover for Japanese bomber planes and to shoot down American planes.

the course of the Japanese Midway invasion force, then Nagumo must be somewhere to the northeast of Midway. Fletcher kept heading in that direction, ready to ambush Nagumo when the moment was right. As Fletcher said later: "After a battle is over, people talk a lot about how the decisions were methodically reached, but actually there's always . . . a lot of groping around."

About 4:00 A.M. on June 4, 1942, the Japanese pilots on Nagumo's carriers were awake. The First Carrier Striking Force was in position, and the pilots were eager to begin their assault on Midway. Led by Lieutenant Joichi Tomonaga, a veteran of the attack on Pearl Harbor, the Japanese pilots were airborne in less than an hour. The assault force included high-level bombers that would strike the American antiaircraft positions at Midway. Then the dive-bombers would swoop in and hit the enemy's troops and ground installations. Japanese Zeros would provide fighter cover for the bombers and knock the American planes out of the skies. While more than 100 planes headed for Midway, Admiral Nagumo kept some of his aircraft in reserve. He was not sure whether an American fleet was somewhere in the area, and, if so, whether that fleet included carriers. Nagumo sent out a few patrol planes to search for the enemy. But the planes were late getting started, and there were not enough of them to do a complete scouting job. The Japanese were reluctant to send aircraft on patrol missions that could be used as part of the assault on the enemy. This would prove costly later in the battle. As one high ranking Japanese officer put it: "It has to be admitted that the planning of the air searching itself was slipshod. It should have been planned more mathematically."

As the Japanese approached Midway, American patrol planes were already in the air and reporting the enemy position back to Midway. By 6:00 A.M., U.S. planes were taxiing down the runways. No one wanted a repeat of Pearl Harbor or the Philippines where the American planes were caught on the ground. As the Japanese planes drew in sight of Midway, they were unexpectedly struck by the American fighters. The initial advantage went to the American fighter pilots when they destroyed two Japanese bombers. But the Zeros quickly rebounded. These planes were much faster and far more maneuverable than anything the Americans could put in the air. The Japanese pilots were also more experienced. Although the Americans put up a brave fight, the enemy was too much for them, shooting many of the American fighters out of the sky.

Meanwhile, Japanese bombers were hitting Midway. They knocked out the mess hall, an airplane hangar, and a powerhouse. Zeros swooped down, strafing oil tanks and setting off tremendous fires. The Japanese attack produced considerable damage on Midway, but there were few American casualties. The U.S. troops had been well dug in and avoided being hit by the enemy planes. As the Japanese turned westward to return to their carriers, just after 7:00 A.M., Lieutenant Tomonaga realized that their mission had not been completed. None of the American planes had been caught on the runways, and the forces on Midway were still capable of putting up a strong defense. Tomonaga immediately contacted Admiral Nagumo: "There is need for a second attack."

Nagumo now faced a difficult decision. He still did not know whether an American flotilla, possibly with several aircraft carriers, lurked somewhere near enough to strike his ships. If he immediately launched a second strike against Midway with the planes still aboard his carriers, they would be completely undefended when the Americans attacked. Yet one of his major assignments was to soften up Midway so it could not withstand a Japanese invasion. As Nagumo was trying to decide on a plan, American aircraft were suddenly spotted approaching his carrier task force. These were torpedo bombers from Midway. They flew in low, dropped their torpedoes into the water and hoped they would speed toward a Japanese aircraft carrier and destroy it. But the bombers had to attack in the face of ferocious enemy antiaircraft fire, as well as dogged pursuit by Japanese Zeros that knocked many of the American planes out of the sky. The Japanese defense proved strong enough to prevent any of Nagumo's carriers from being damaged.

After the American attack, however, Admiral Nagumo decided that he must launch another strike at Midway before the planes stationed there did any more damage. Nagumo's bombers on board the carriers had been armed with torpedoes specially designed to sink ships if the American carriers had attacked him. He immediately ordered that the armaments on the planes be changed to bombs that would create the maximum amount of destruction to the ground installations on Midway. Shortly after the order was given, however, Admiral Nagumo received a report from one of his patrol planes. It had spotted enemy ships. There was an American flotilla in the vicinity, after all. Nagumo changed his order. The planes being fitted to attack Midway must be refitted to strike the American fleet.

As the Japanese planes were being refitted, another squadron of American dive-bombers appeared at about 8:00 A.M. These were led by Major Lofton Henderson from Midway. The bombers came in with no fighter protection so they were easy targets for the Zeros, which swooped down on them. Although the gunners in the American planes tried to fight them off, the Zeros were much too fast. Once again, the American pilots failed to hit the Japanese carriers. As the attack continued, Admiral Nagumo was getting more information from his patrol planes. They had seen American cruisers and destroyers, but no carriers. Perhaps the Japanese could concentrate on Midway, after all, and launch another attack against the islands.

But Nagumo had to deal with another problem first. Another American squadron was heading toward his fleet. Colonel Walter Sweeney, who had led his bombers against the Japanese invasion force on June 3, was making a run at the Japanese carriers. Unlike the dive-bombers, the B-17s dropped their bombs from thousands of feet in the air. Unfortunately, for Sweeney's pilots, none of the bombs scored a direct hit. Once again, the Japanese carriers had escaped unscathed. The American military leaders were not yet experienced enough to mount a coordinated assault including fighters, high level bombers, dive-bombers, and torpedo planes. As a result, the U.S. attacks were not effective. As Admiral Nimitz, himself, admitted. "Although the [torpedo plane] is a well armed plane, it is obvious that it cannot go through fighter opposition without fighter protection."

As the Japanese were defending themselves against the latest assaults, a new message came in from a patrol plane.

The Japanese pilots caused enormous damage at Midway by setting off oil tank fires.

It had spotted an American carrier along with the other enemy ships to the east. Suddenly, Admiral Nagumo faced another difficult decision. He could launch an attack against the American carriers with the planes that were already outfitted with armaments aimed at ships. But if these planes were launched, it might spell disaster for Lieutenant Tomonaga's force, which was already circling overhead after its initial raid on Midway. These planes were running out of fuel and would have to ditch in the ocean if they were not allowed to land. However, if

Aircraft at Midway

American Aircraft

Bombers	B-17s (Flying Fortresses)
Torpedo Planes	B-26s
	TBDs
	TBFs
Patrol Planes	PBYs
Dive Bombers	SBDs
	Vindicators (stationed on Midway)
Fighters	F4Fs
	Buffalos (stationed on Midway)

Japanese Aircraft

Fighters	Zeros
Bombers	
Dive Bombers	

Nagumo waited for them to land, he might lose valuable time to launch his attack. The same thing might happen if he waited to rearm all his planes with bombs designed to sink the enemy carriers. If the American carrier task force had somehow discovered his position, it might gain the initiative and launch its planes first.

A debate raged among Nagumo's top officers. Rear Admiral Tamon Yamaguchi, who commanded the aircraft carrier *Hiryu* was in favor of an immediate strike with every available plane, no matter what type of armament it carried. And he was not prepared to wait for the fighters to escort them. But Chief of Staff Rear Admiral Ryunosuke Kusaka disagreed. He wanted to give Tomonaga an opportunity to land and refuel. Without this fighter support, Kusaka reasoned, the Japanese bombers would be easy targets, just as the American bombers had been when they attacked the Japanese fleet. Nagumo decided to take the extra time necessary to launch a coordinated attack. This had always proven successful for the Japanese in the past.

What Nagumo did not realize was that Admiral Spruance and Admiral Fletcher were already aware of his approximate position and had decided to strike. The American commanders had planned a well-timed assault with bombers, fighters, and torpedo planes. However, the Japanese fleet was still about 150 miles from the U.S. carrier flotilla. This meant that the fighters and torpedo planes might not have enough gas to go out, fight, and return to the carriers. After the pilots parachuted into the ocean they would be picked up by American ships. Nevertheless, Spruance and Fletcher were convinced that they must hit the Japanese before the enemy was aware that the Americans were there. In addition, Spruance decided to hit the Japanese as hard as possible using every plane he had available.

At approximately, 7:00 A.M., the planes began to take off from Spruance's carriers, the *Hornet* and the *Enterprise*. Spruance knew about the Japanese attack on Midway. He hoped to time his strike against the enemy carriers shortly after their planes had returned and were sitting on the decks of their carriers.

The planes from the *Enterprise* were led by Commander Wade McClusky. His dive-bombers were the first to take off. They circled, waiting for the torpedo planes and fighters. But there were delays on board the carrier getting the other planes in the air. Finally, McClusky was told to leave with the dive-bombers, and the other aircraft would follow him, hopefully rendezvousing before the strike. At about the same time, torpedo squadrons were also taking off from the *Hornet*. But there seemed to be little coordination between the contingents from the two carriers. In addition, the dive-bombers as well as the fighter support from the *Hornet,* which was supposed to cover a contingent of torpedo planes, missed them in the clouds. Some of these planes never found the enemy.

Between 9:15 and 9:30, one squadron of torpedo planes, under the command of John Waldron, began their attack. Once again, the American planes were unequal to the Zeros. Waldron's own aircraft was raked by enemy bullets and caught fire. The other planes in the squadron were also hit, without causing any damage to the Japanese carriers. A few minutes later, another group of torpedo planes attacked the Japanese flotilla. Led by Colonel Gene Lindsey, these planes had hoped to wait for support from American fighters. But they were nowhere in sight. What's more, Lindsey's planes were starting to run low on fuel. So he had no choice but to launch an attack. More than two dozen Japanese Zeros struck the torpedo planes and knocked many of them out of sky. The rest kept flying toward the Japanese carriers, hoping to release their torpedoes and sink the enemy ships. But it was no use—another American attack had failed.

As the American planes from Admiral Spruance's flotilla struck the Japanese, Admiral Fletcher was moving his own ships, including the carrier *Yorktown,* closer and closer to Admiral Nagumo's carriers. Fletcher decided that he would launch some of his planes, but also leave some in reserve. The torpedo planes were the first to take off, followed by the dive-bombers and the fighters. Shortly after 10:00 A.M., they began to see the Japanese ships. But by this time, the enemy Zeros had also spotted the Americans. The Japanese swooped down on the torpedo planes. Meanwhile, other Zeros attacked the American fighters, so the pilots could not support each other. The torpedo planes were left on their own and were destroyed before they could do any damage to the enemy.

The attack was over soon after 10 A.M. The Japanese

American Naval Commanders

Rear Admiral Frank Jack Fletcher: Task Force 17

Fletcher was born in Iowa in 1885 and graduated from the Naval Academy at Annapolis, Maryland, in 1906. After serving on several battle-ships, he participated in the American occupation of Vera Cruz, Mexico in 1914. During this operation, he won the Medal of Honor for rescuing people fleeing from a Mexican ship in the area. During World War I, he commanded the USS *Benham,* which guarded American supply ships crossing the Atlantic. After the war, Fletcher served in various posts, including Chief of Staff to the Commander in Chief, U.S. Atlantic Fleet, aide to the Secretary of the Navy, and finally commander of cruisers in the Pacific from 1939 until the attack on Pearl Harbor. After commanding American ships at the Battle of the Coral Sea in May 1942, he returned to Hawaii.

Admiral Raymond Spruance was born in 1886 and graduated from the Naval Academy in 1906. He then went on to command destroyers and eventually the battleship *Mississippi.* At the outbreak of World War II, he was in charge of the American fleet in the Caribbean area. Spruance was a very understated man and avoided the limelight whenever he could. After his role in the Battle of Midway, he said: "There were a hundred Spruances in the Navy. They just happened to pick me for the job."

had beaten everything that the enemy had been able to hurl at them. So far, the Battle of Midway looked like a Japanese victory. But there was more to come. Unfortunately for Nagumo, his patrol planes had not spotted the American carriers soon enough. Otherwise, he might not have wasted so much time arming and rearming his planes. Instead, they would have been prepared to take off toward the enemy much sooner and delivered a strike far earlier. Instead, the initiative passed from the Japanese to the Americans. As one expert has explained, Midway "was an Intelligence failure." Precious time lost early in the battle would now tip the scales in favor of the United States.

Destroying Japanese Aircraft Carriers

On June 4, 1942, crewmen climbed down ropes and ladders to board boats that would take them to rescue ships after the aircraft carrier *Yorktown* was hit by Japanese bombers.

Southward from the battle raging around the Japanese aircraft carriers, Lieutenant Commander Wade McClusky, who had led his dive-bombers off the deck of the *Enterprise,* was still searching for the enemy fleet. It was almost ten o'clock and his planes were running low on gas and would have to return home unless they found the Japanese carriers soon. Suddenly, McClusky saw something—a Japanese ship heading northward. Following it, McClusky finally came upon what he had been looking for all along: Admiral Nagumo's task force.

Lieutenant Clarence E. Dickinson, flying in McClusky's squadron, described what lay 20,000 feet below them, spread out along the Pacific Ocean. "I could see two long, narrow, yellow rectangles, the flight decks of carriers . . . Then farther off I saw a third carrier. I had expected to see only two and when I saw the third my heart went lower. The southwest corner of the fleet's position was obscured by a storm area. Suddenly another long yellow rectangle came sliding out of that obscurity. A fourth carrier!"

McClusky expected to see Japanese Zeros swooping in to attack his dive-bombers. But the Zeros were still flying at low levels, after fighting off the previous American attacks. As a result, McClusky had a clear path to attack the carriers. The bombers began to dive toward the two largest Japanese carriers, the *Kaga* and the *Akagi*. Lieutenant Dickinson gave the signal to the other planes in his division and they swooped down out of the sky headed toward the giant enemy carriers. Bombs hit the water next to the *Kaga,* then struck the carrier itself.

Unknown to McClusky, another squadron of planes was attacking the Japanese carriers at exactly the same time. The dive-bombers from the American carrier *Yorktown* had also spotted the enemy and were preparing to strike. Led by Lieutenant Commander Max Leslie, the bombers headed for the huge carrier *Kaga*. They scored a direct hit, creating havoc on the *Kaga*. According to one report:

> There was a tremendous burst of fire near the super-structure. Pieces of the *Kaga's* flight deck whirled in the air; a Zero taking off into the wind was blown into the sea; the bridge [command center] was a shambles of twisted metal, shattered glass and bodies. . . . Then came three more vicious explosions, hurling planes over the side, tearing huge holes in the flight deck and starting fires which spread to the hangar deck below. Screaming sailors ran around aimlessly, trailing flames. Officers shouted orders against the

deafening blasts. Gasoline poured from the planes' ruptured fuel tanks, and some of the pilots who had not been lucky enough to escape the first bomb blast were cremated at their controls.

The American bombers had caught the Japanese carriers with their planes preparing to take off against the American carriers that had been located to the north. Meanwhile, McClusky's planes were attacking the *Akagi* and the *Soryu*. On these ships, the Japanese aircraft were also nearly ready to be launched against U.S. ships. As the bombs fell from the American planes, they scored direct hits on the enemy targets. The *Akagi's* flight deck was hit, destroying planes and killing pilots. Below deck, the *Akagi's* hangar was blown up; planes caught fire, killing many Japanese sailors.

The *Akagi* was Admiral Nagumo's flagship. As it became clear that the giant carrier was going to sink, his officers urged him to leave the *Akagi* so he could continue commanding the battle from another ship. "Sir, our radio is smashed and we cannot communicate with the other ships," they told him. "Should you not transfer your command to another vessel so that you can continue to direct the battle?" But Nagumo stubbornly wanted to remain aboard his ship. As the fires spread, his chief of staff, Admiral Ryunosuke Kusaka, ordered several of his subordinates to forcibly remove Nagumo from the *Akagi* and transfer him to another vessel.

The same scene of death and destruction was being repeated aboard the third Japanese carrier, the *Soryu*. As naval historian Samuel Eliot Morison wrote: "At 10.24 Japan had been on top; six minutes later, on that bright June morning, three of her big carriers were on their flaming way to death." The deck of the *Soryu* was on fire, explosions were heard everywhere, and sailors were jumping overboard into the sea to save their lives. However, the ship's captain, Ryusaku Yanigimoto, would not leave his ship. He died as the bridge was covered in flames. Although the carriers did not sink immediately, there was no question of their ultimate fate. The fires continued throughout the rest of the day. That evening, the *Soryu* sank, followed by the *Kaga,* and finally the next morning, the *Akagi.* Three Japanese destroyers finished off the *Akagi* when it was clear that the ship could not be saved, sending torpedoes into it. Aboard the destroyer, sailors yelled, "*Akagi* banzai, banzai, and banzai!"

Far to the west, Admiral Yamamoto began to receive reports of what had happened to his magnificent fleet. First he had heard about fire aboard the *Akagi,* then about the damage to the *Soryu* and the *Kagi.* Unfortunately, the Japanese admiral had remained too far to the rear to support Admiral Nagumo's fleet. Yamamoto had decided to split his forces. If he had been closer, his destroyers and cruisers might have been able to bring more antiaircraft fire to bear on the American bombers, preventing them from doing so much damage to the Japanese carrier task force.

One Japanese carrier, however, still remained. The carrier *Hiryu* was northward and escaped the American onslaught that had destroyed the other ships. Admiral Tamon Yamaguchi ordered the planes aboard the *Hiryu* to take off immediately and attack the American fleet that lay to the northeast. Eighteen dive-bombers along with a small number of Zero fighter planes took off from the flight deck of the *Hiryu* to launch one last desperate strike. Led by Lieutenant Michio Kobayashi, a combat veteran, the planes were headed for the *Yorktown*, which had been located by Japanese patrol planes.

Aboard the *Yorktown,* Admiral Fletcher had already received word that his planes had knocked out three of the Japanese carriers. In fact, many of these planes were already returning home and some had landed. At approximately noon, however, the ship's radar began picking up approaching Japanese planes. The rest of the American planes were

Japanese bomber planes torpedoed the USS *Yorktown*. The carrier tried to evade the attack and fired back at the enemy planes, but the damage to the ship was too great for the ship to stay afloat.

told to stay in the air and away from the carrier. The destroyers nearby moved in to help the *Yorktown* fend off the coming attack. As the Japanese planes drew closer, they were suddenly attacked by American fighter planes that shot some of them out of the sky.

What was left of Lieutenant Kobayashi's task force continued to head for the *Yorktown*. There were less than half his dive-bombers still flying, but that might be enough. As the Japanese planes swooped down on the *Yorktown*, it tried evasive action, turning in one direction then another to avoid being hit by torpedoes. And the carrier's guns kept firing back at the oncoming Japanese planes. But the pilots dropped their torpedoes and two of them found their mark. Explosions ripped the insides of the *Yorktown*, and the ship was no longer able to keep moving.

In the distance, Admiral Spruance aboard the carrier *Enterprise* sent cruisers and destroyers from his task force to assist Fletcher. But several of the Japanese planes escaped, radioed a report back to the *Hiryu,* and flew back to the carrier to refuel. Since the first attack had been successful, the Japanese decided to launch another one. Initially, they believed that only the *Yorktown* would be their target. But new intelligence coming in from the Japanese patrol planes included sightings of two additional carriers—the *Enterprise* and the *Hornet.*

Although the *Hiryu* had only a few remaining fighters and torpedo planes, Admiral Yamaguchi directed them to take off and attack the enemy. This squadron was led by Lieutenant Joichi Tomonaga, whose planes had struck Midway at the beginning of the battle. Aboard the *Yorktown,* repairmen were working hard to fix the damage. They rapidly repaired a hole on the flight deck, covering it with beams and metal plates. Medical personnel tried to save some of the men who had been injured in the attack. But many others lay dead throughout the ship. Below deck, smoke poured out of the boiler rooms and the carrier was unable to move. After about an hour, several boilers were finally repaired and the *Yorktown* could make slow progress through the water. However, Admiral Fletcher had not stayed aboard the carrier while the work was completed. He had already moved to another ship, the cruiser *Astoria,* from which he could continue to direct the battle.

By mid-afternoon, Tomonaga had reached the vicinity of the *Yorktown* and prepared to begin his attack. But the Japanese planes were not going to have an easy time. American fighters dove out of the sky and struck

Tomonaga's planes. From the sea below, the Japanese were hit with heavy antiaircraft fire from the American ships. But their planes kept coming toward the *Yorktown*. Flying very low over the water, the pilots dropped their torpedoes. The *Yorktown* tried to turn quickly enough to avoid them. But it was no use. Suddenly, one torpedo hit the carrier, then another one struck. "There were muffled explosions, like rolling thunder, and it seemed to those on deck that the *Yorktown* had been lifted a foot or two out of the water. Paint flew off the bulkheads [sides of the ship], books toppled from their racks, and electrical power failed, plunging the lower decks into darkness. The whine of the generators petered out." Once again, the *Yorktown* was dead in the water, and the ship began to tip dangerously. Water was pouring into the lower decks. The captain of the *Yorktown* realized that the ship could not be saved this time. "Pass the word to abandon ship," he told his crew. The American sailors went over the side, some swimming and others in life boats.

Those in the water had a particularly difficult time. As historian Jeff Nesmith wrote: "The torpedoes [from the Japanese planes] had broken open fuel tanks on the port [left] side and tons of fuel oil oozed out onto the surface. Soon the ship was surrounded by a huge oil slick. Sailors had to swim through it. Many gulped oil and became wretchedly ill in the water. Others were sickened by the fumes." Some sailors helped their comrades who had been wounded. Eventually, more than 2,000 men were picked up by nearby U.S. destroyers.

Having put the *Yorktown* out of action, the remaining Japanese planes left the battle and returned to the carrier *Hiryu*. Admiral Fletcher was determined that this fourth enemy carrier, which had accounted for the destruction of the *Yorktown,* must not be allowed to get away. While the *Yorktown* was being attacked, an American patrol

American planes bombed the *Hiryu*, sinking it during the decisive Battle of Midway.

plane spotted the position of the *Hiryu*. It was now up to Admiral Spruance, commanding the *Enterprise* and *Hornet,* to launch another attack that might destroy the last remaining enemy carrier. However, Spruance was short of planes following the earlier futile attacks against the Japanese carriers. He could send out only a small number of dive-bombers and torpedo planes. These headed for the *Hiryu*.

Meanwhile, aboard the last Japanese carrier, Admiral Yamaguchi was preparing another attack with the few planes he still had left. So the pilots would be at their best, he decided to let them rest from their last attack and launch the next one at about 6:00 P.M. It would prove to be a mistake. About an hour before launch time, American planes struck the *Hiryu*. Although the American pilots were attacked by Japanese Zeros and antiaircraft fire, the dive-bombers dropped their payloads. The carrier tried to avoid the bombs, but it was no use. The ship was hit repeatedly. Fires and explosions swept across the *Hiryu*. The carrier and its escort ships were also hit by bombers sent out from Midway. The *Hiryu* burned through the night and finally sank the next morning around 9:00 A.M. Admiral Yamaguchi decided to stay on board and went down with his ship.

Turning Point
in the Pacific

U.S. soldiers are shown standing with the flag-draped bodies of servicemen who died at Midway.

The main Japanese fleet with the giant battleship *Yamato* and Admiral Yamamoto steamed eastward across the Pacific Ocean on the afternoon of June 4, 1942. Although he realized that the odds were long that the Japanese might recover from their losses in the Battle of Midway, Yamamoto was an old poker player who realized that the game was not over until the last card had been played. Messages had been sent out to Admiral Kakuta, supporting the invasion of the Aleutians, to head southward with his two small carriers and escort vessels. Yamamoto had also ordered Admiral Kondo to head northward from his invasion of the Midway Islands. Both of these squadrons would join Admiral Nagumo and, together with Yamamoto's fleet, hit the Americans again. In addition, Admiral Yamamoto believed that Japan had lost only three large carriers. The *Hiryu,* he confidently thought, was still operational and could launch planes against the enemy.

At 5:30 P.M., however, Yamamoto received the somber news that the *Hiryu* was burning after being hit by American planes. He was stunned—the devastation to his glorious navy had been far greater than he could have imagined. But Admiral Nagumo was still not ready to give up. He was planning a night attack against the American ships. This would blunt the impact of their aircraft carriers and planes, which could not be effective in the dark. Then Nagumo received a report from one of his patrol planes that the Americans still had four carriers in operation. Although the information was mistaken, it was enough for Nagumo. He decided that his decimated squadron had to retreat westward.

Admiral Yamamoto, however, was still not prepared to break off the battle. He issued another report directing Nagumo and Kondo to prepare to engage the enemy on the following day. Admiral Kondo was already heading north-ward and hoped to be able to begin a new attack during the night. With his large battleships, Kondo believed he might inflict enough damage on the American fleet to at least partially avenge the terrible loss of the four carriers.

As Admiral Kondo was moving into position, Admiral Spruance had decided on a different course of action. Although the Americans had scored a stunning victory on June 4, Spruance was not certain that the Japanese would call off their invasion of Midway. Therefore, he decided to head east so he could be near the islands in case of attack. Spruance also realized that the American fleet was out-numbered by Yamamoto's combined forces, so he didn't want to risk his ships by heading west and engaging the enemy. He and Admiral Fletcher commanded the only battle-worthy squadrons in the Pacific, so they could not afford to risk having them lost. Fletcher was content with the victory he had already won and did not want to engage what was left of the Japanese Imperial fleet.

By the early morning of June 5, Admiral Yamamoto had decided to accept the inevitable. Admiral Kondo could not begin a night battle with the enemy soon enough to do any significant damage before daylight arrived and the Americans could launch planes from their carriers. Therefore, Yamamoto directed Kondo and Nagumo to head west and join the main Japanese fleet. He also sent a message to Admiral Takeo Kurita, who had been directed to renew the attack on Midway, to turn around and head west. But as two of his large cruisers, the *Mikuma* and the *Mogami,* maneuvered in the darkness, they collided. The *Mogami* suffered serious damage and her progress through the sea was slow.

News of the *Mogami's* problems was radioed to Midway by an American submarine that had been trailing Admiral Kurita's fleet. Dive-bombers were sent out and they attacked the *Mogami* and the *Mikuma* shortly after 8:00 A.M. on the morning of June 5. One American plane smashed into the *Mikuma,* causing serious fires aboard the ship. Nevertheless, the crew of the *Mikuma* succeeded in containing the damage, and both ships kept on course.

Meanwhile, Admiral Spruance had been monitoring the reports of the Japanese fleet and realized it was heading westward away from Midway. He had also been told that one large carrier still remained afloat (the *Hiryu* did not sink until approximately 9:00 A.M.). So Spruance ordered his squadron to turn around and slowly head west. He was prepared to follow the Japanese but not too closely because he did not want to get ambushed by Admiral Yamamoto's superior fleet. During the afternoon of June 5, Spruance launched dive-bombers from his two aircraft carriers, the *Hornet* and the *Enterprise.* Although they searched for the enemy over several hours, they only spotted one destroyer,

the *Tanikaze*. The Japanese commander Motomi Katsumi
was skilled enough to maneuver his ship so it was not hit by
the American bombers. By this time the American planes
were running low on fuel and returned east to their carriers.

Farther westward lay the entire Japanese fleet. The
ships were now approximately 350 miles from Midway.
Admirals Nagumo, Kurita, and Kondo had joined Admiral
Yamamoto well beyond the range of the American carriers
and their planes. The Japanese navy was finally safe from
attack. That is, all except the crippled *Mogami* and *Mikuma*
and a couple of destroyers that were accompanying them.
On the morning of June 6, they were struck by successive
waves of American planes from the *Hornet* and the
Enterprise. The Japanese cruisers were not being protected
by Zeros, so they were hit repeatedly. Sailors aboard the
Mikuma began to abandon ship, and the cruiser eventually
sank in the evening. However, the *Mogami* was not damaged
as badly and survived the attack.

While this battle was underway, American repairmen
were trying to save the giant carrier *Yorktown*, which had
been crippled during the main engagement on June 4.
While the men worked, American destroyers hovered near
the *Yorktown* while keeping a lookout for enemy submarines. One Japanese sub actually was in the area. *I-168,*
under the command of Lieutenant Commander Yahachi
Tanabe, had been patrolling off Midway when it had been
ordered to head for the damaged *Yorktown*, which had been
spotted by a Japanese patrol plane. Tanabe first located the
Yorktown at about 4:00 A.M. on June 6. But he had to be
extremely careful. He did not want his submarine to be seen
by American destroyers because they might sink it with
depth charges. Throughout the morning, he crept closer
and closer to the *Yorktown*. Eventually, he closed to about
1,500 meters, which was an excellent distance from which to
launch his torpedoes. If he had been too close, the torpedoes

would have gone under the *Yorktown,* not into its bulk-heads. If he had been too far away, the torpedoes would not have hit with their full force. Tanabe looked through his periscope and realized the enemy carrier was in a perfect position for him to inflict the maximum damage.

Tanabe gave the order to fire. Four torpedoes cut through the water, heading for the target. American sailors aboard the *Yorktown* saw them coming but there was little they could do. The carrier was hit, along with the destroyer *Hammann.* The destroyer sunk rapidly, within four minutes, after breaking apart. But as she sunk, her own depth charges exploded and sailors who had abandoned ship were killed in the water. As one survivor reported: "All those heads that had been on the water just before the depth charges exploded suddenly disappeared, something like a windshield wiper erases the droplets from your windshield when it's raining. They were all gone."

Two torpedoes also hit the *Yorktown* and sailors began to abandon ship, but they had far more time than the men aboard the *Hammann.* The carrier stayed afloat throughout the afternoon and evening, although there was nothing that could be done to rescue it. Finally, at approximately 5:00 A.M. on June 7, 1942, the great carrier sunk. Meanwhile, Tanabe had been trying to escape the American destroyers that were coming after him. Shortly after launching his torpedoes, the depth charges from the destroyers began exploding near his submarine, but it escaped a direct hit. As he piloted his submarine away, however, it lost electric power after depth charges had been discharged nearby. Then air pressure in the sub began to decline as it was forced to remain under water. If the pressure got too low, Tanabe and his men would die.

Eventually, Tanabe decided to take a chance and come to the surface. As he looked around, there were no enemy ships in the vicinity. But in the distance he spotted several

American destroyers. They apparently saw him, too, because they began heading in his direction. The submarine submerged again and this time Tanabe succeeded in evading his pursuers. He had also informed command headquarters that he had sunk the *Yorktown*. It was the only good news the Japanese had received throughout the entire battle.

By the time the *Yorktown* went down, the Battle of Midway had ended. On the evening of June 6, Admiral Spruance had already decided to head eastward. The *Hiryu* had sunk, so there was no further need to engage the Japanese. Admiral Yamamoto had also officially broken off the engagement.

For the Japanese, Midway had been a devastating defeat. More than 2,100 men were killed, three times the number of casualties sustained by the American forces. The Japanese had also lost 4 large carriers and over 300 aircraft, to 1 carrier and approximately 150 planes for the United States. Japan's high command attributed its defeat to several causes. As one high ranking officer put it: "All in all, we can't help concluding that the main cause for the defeat was that we had become conceited with past success and lacked studies of what to do in case an enemy air force appears on a flank while we are launching a concentrated attack." This is exactly what happened. The Japanese, believing because of their earlier victories in the Pacific that they were invincible, had underestimated the abilities of the Americans.

Perhaps it was also Japanese conceit that prevented them from sending out enough patrol planes to find the position of the American carriers before the invasion of Midway began. In addition, the Japanese high command did not dispatch an effective patrol of submarines to scout out the position of the enemy. Admiral Nagumo was criticized after the battle for waiting too long to launch his attack against the American carriers. Instead of keeping his planes on the carriers until they were all outfitted with torpedoes, he might have sent them against the American carriers, even though some of his aircraft were equipped with bombs that were designed to be dropped on Midway. Although these might not have done as much damage to the carriers, any attack would have been better than nothing. Instead, the Japanese carriers were caught with the planes still aboard them, and they were destroyed.

But, in Nagumo's defense, he found himself in a difficult situation. He had been given two assignments: to attack Midway and to find and destroy the American fleet. It was really impossible for him to accomplish both missions. Admiral Yamamoto had not designed the Japanese attack plan carefully. In splitting Nagumo's targets, Yamamoto had almost set up Nagumo to fail. Indeed, the main fault for Midway has usually been attributed by historians to Admiral Yamamoto. By dividing his forces, he kept his large battleships too far to the rear where they could not help Admiral Nagumo fend off the American aerial attack. Yamamoto further weakened his flotilla by sending part of it to assault the Aleutian Islands. This diversion did not fool the American high command, but it did reduce the power of the main Japanese strike force.

Of course, Admiral Yamamoto did not know that American intelligence had broken the Japanese code and knew his plans. While this was a major reason for the American victory at the Battle of Midway, it was not enough to assure a victory. During the first hours of the battle, the American high command sent a series of uncoordinated air attacks against the Japanese that proved completely ineffective. Indeed, by 10:15 A.M. on June 4, Admiral Nagumo had been winning the battle and was preparing to send his planes against the American carriers. Fortunately, the American dive-bombers found the Japanese carriers just as the enemy was ending the last attack on the U.S. torpedo planes. Since the Zeroes were out of position to fire on the

These Avenger torpedo bombers were used by the United States at the Battle of Midway. The pilots were able to hit Japanese carriers and destroy the aircraft on deck.

approaching American planes, the Americans were successful in hitting the Japanese carriers and catching the enemy's aircraft on the carrier decks.

It was an American stroke of luck. But it was due in part to the decision by Admiral Spruance to send everything he had against the Japanese. Had he held back some of his planes, the air attack would not have been so successful. As naval historian Samuel Eliot Morison wrote, "Spruance's performance was superb. Calm, collected, decisive, yet receptive to advice; keeping in his mind the picture of widely disparate forces, yet boldly seizing every opening, Raymond A. Spruance emerged from this battle one of the greatest admirals in American naval history." Not only did

Spruance strike decisively, he also knew when to call off the battle and not pursue the enemy. This prevented his fleet from being beaten in a night attack by Yamamoto's vastly superior naval force.

The victory of the American navy at Midway had far reaching effects on the entire war in the Pacific. As military historian John Keegan put it: "Within exactly five minutes, between 10.25 and 10.30, the whole course of the war in the Pacific had been reversed. [Nagumo's] Fleet, its magnificent ships, modern aircraft and superb pilots, had been devastated." By contrast, if the Japanese had won the Battle of Midway, they might have established a forward position in the Pacific. From Midway, they might have launched another attack on Pearl Harbor and successfully occupied Hawaii.

From this point on, however, the Japanese would be on the defensive in the Pacific Ocean. Although more carriers would be built in Japan, far more would be produced by the industrial might of the United States. Admiral Yamamoto had predicted that the Japanese had about six months of "running wild," as he put it, in the Pacific before the United States would recover. Pearl Harbor had occurred on December 7, 1941, almost exactly six months before the Japanese defeat at Midway. As Admiral Nimitz explained: "Pearl Harbor has now been partially avenged. Vengeance will not be complete until Japanese sea power has been reduced to impotence."

The American advance across the Pacific would now begin. The victory at Midway had greatly improved U.S. morale and enabled American commanders to realize that they could beat the Japanese. By contrast, Admiral Yamamoto had to go on the defensive and fight against the United States much nearer the Japanese homeland. Over the next three years, the Japanese empire would steadily shrink against the onslaught of superior American military power until the Americans were victorious in 1945.

1853	Commodore Matthew Perry arrives in Edo Bay, Japan
1895	Japanese destroy Chinese fleet
1898	United States defeats Spain in Spanish-American War; American forces occupy Spanish colony of the Philippines
1899	Secretary of State John Hay announces Open Door policy in China
1905	Japanese defeat Russian fleet at Battle of Tsushima Straits
1907-9	President Theodore Roosevelt sends Great White Fleet around the world
1910	Japan takes control of Korea
1921	Washington Naval Conference limits size of naval fleets
1932	Japanese take control of Manchuria
1937	Japanese massacre civilians in Nanking, China
1939	Japan occupies every major city in China; Nazi German invades Poland, beginning World War II

1905
Japanese defeat
Russian fleet
at Battle of
Tsushima Straits

1910
Japan takes control
of Korea

1939
Japan occupies every
major city in China

1937
Japanese massacre
civilians in
Nanking, China

1932
Japanese take
control of
Manchuria

Timeline

1940	Nazis overrun most of western Europe
1941	
December 7	Japanese attack Pearl Harbor; Japanese planes bomb the Philippines
December 8	United States declares war on Japan
December 10	Japanese planes sink British ships, *Prince of Wales* and *Repulse*
December 21	Japan invades Philippines
December 25	Japan takes control of Hong Kong
December 31	Admiral Nimitz becomes commander of U.S. Pacific Fleet
1942	
February 15	British fortress of Singapore in Malaya surrenders to Japan
March 6	Japanese capture Batavia, capital of Dutch East Indies
April 9	Bataan surrenders in the Philippines

December 25
Japan takes control of Hong Kong

December 21
Japan invades Philippines

April 18
American planes led by James Doolitle bomb Japanese cities

April 9
Bataan surrenders in the Philippines

June 3-5
Battle of Midway

June 3
Japanese invade Aleutian Islands

June 3
American planes bomb Japanese invasion convoy

June 4
American planes destroy four large Japanese carriers

June 4
Japanese planes damage American carrier *Yorktown*

June 5
Japanese call off battle and retreat; *Yorktown* sunk by Japanese submarine

1941   1942

December 7
Japanese attack Pearl Harbor

December 7
Japanese planes bomb the Philippines

December 10
Japanese planes sink British ships, *Prince of Wales* and *Repulse*

February 15
British fortress of Singapore in Malaya surrenders to Japan

March 6
Japanese capture Batavia, capital of Dutch East Indies

May 7, 8
U.S. and Japanese ships fight at Battle of Coral Sea

May 6
Corregidor surrenders; Japanese control the Philippines

April 18	American planes led by James Doolitle bomb Japanese cities
May 6	Corregidor surrenders; Japanese control the Philippines
May 7, 8	U.S. and Japanese ships fight at Battle of Coral Sea
June 3	Japanese invade Aleutian Islands
June 3-5	Battle of Midway
June 3	American planes bomb Japanese invasion convoy
June 4	American planes destroy four large Japanese carriers; Japanese planes damage American carrier *Yorktown*
June 5	Japanese call off battle and retreat; *Yorktown* sunk by Japanese submarine

Caffrey, Kate. *Out in the Midday Sun: Singapore 1941-45—The End of an Empire.* New York: Stein and Day, 1973.

Calvocoressi, Peter, et al. *Total War: The Causes and Courses of the Second World War.* New York: Pantheon Books, 1989.

Cook, Haruko Taya and Cook, Theodore F. *Japan at War: An Oral History.* New York: The New Press, 1992.

Henshall, Kenneth G. *A History of Japan: From Stone Age to Superpower.* New York: St. Martin's Press, 1999.

Hoyt, Edwin. *Warlord: Tojo Against the World.* Lanham, Maryland: Scarborough House, 1993.

Kahn, David. *The Codebreakers: The Story of Secret Writing.* New York: Scribner's, 1996.

Keegan, John. *The Second World War.* New York: Viking, 1989.

Millett, Allan R. and Maslowski, Peter. *For the Common Defense: A Military History of the United States of America.* New York: Free Press, 1984.

Morison, Samuel Eliot and Commager, Henry Steele. *The Growth of the American Republic.* New York: Oxford University Press, 1962.

Morison, Samuel Eliot. *The Two-Ocean War: A Short History of the United States Navy in the Second World War.* New York: Galahad Books, 1997.

Nesmith, Jeff. *No Higher Honor.* Atlanta: Longstreet, 1999.

Prange, Gordon W. et al. *Miracle at Midway.* New York: McGraw-Hill, 1982.

Roberson, John R. *Japan: From Shogun to Sony, 1543-1984.* New York, Atheneum, 1985.

Akagi, 57, 78, 79, 80
Aleutian Islands, 11, 56,
   57, 66, 87, 93
Astoria, 82
Australia, 9

Bataan, 43-44, 45
Bataan Death March, 45
Borneo, 45, 50
Burma, 49, 50

Chiang Kai-shek, 25, 26
China
   and Japan, 20-21, 24,
      25-26, 32, 36, 37-38
   and Open Door policy,
      32-33, 35
   and opening to
      Western trade, 18
   and Russia, 21
   and United States,
      30-31, 32-33, 34,
      35, 36
Combat Intelligence Unit,
   12-14
Coral Sea, Battle of the,
   12-13, 53, 59
Corregidor, 44, 45

Dewey, George, 29-30
Dickinson, Clarence E.,
   77-78
Doolittle, James H., 51,
   59
Doorman, Karel, 50
Dutch East Indies, 8, 27,
   41, 50, 51

Enterprise, 59, 73, 77, 82,
   84, 89, 90

Fillmore, Millard, 18
Fletcher, Frank Jack,
   52-53, 59, 60, 62, 66-67,
   73, 74, 80, 82, 83, 88-89

Fourteen Points, 34

Great Depression, 25,
   35-36
Greater East Asia Co-
   Prosperity Sphere,
   50-51
"Great White Fleet,"
   33-34
Guam, 8, 30

Halsey, William F. (Bull),
   59, 60
Hammann, 91
Haramuchi, Nogi, 51
Hawaii, 8, 10, 31-32
   See also Pearl Harbor
Hay, John, 32
Henderson, Lofton, 70
Hirohito, Emperor, 24,
   25, 27
Hiryu, 57, 72, 80, 82, 83,
   84-85, 88, 89, 92
Homma, Masaharu, 43,
   44
Hong Kong, 8, 41, 42-43
Hoover, Herbert, 35
Hornet, 51, 59, 73, 74, 82,
   84, 89, 90
Hull, Cordell, 38

I-168, 90-92
Imperialism, 32
Indochina, 38

Japan
   and Aleutian Islands,
      11, 56, 57, 66, 87, 93
   and Battle of the Coral
      Sea, 53
   and Borneo, 45, 50
   and Burma, 49, 50
   and China, 20-21, 24,
      25-26, 32, 36, 37-38,
      42

and Dutch East Indies,
   8, 27, 41, 50, 51
and expansion, 20,
   24-25
and Hong Kong, 8, 41,
   42-43
and Indochina, 38
and Korea, 21-22
and Malaya, 27, 41, 43,
   45-49
and Manchuria, 21, 22,
   25, 32-33, 35
and Meiji, 19-20, 22
and modernization,
   19-20
and navy, 20, 24, 35,
   36, 50, 56
and 1920s, 24-25
and 1930s, 25
and Pacific, 8-9, 41-51
and Pearl Harbor, 8,
   10, 24, 35, 36-37,
   38-39, 95
and Perry opening
   ports to Western
   trade, 17-19
and Philippines, 8-9,
   41, 42, 43-44
and planes, 43, 44, 50
and Port Moresby,
   12-13, 52-53
and Russia, 21-23
and Singapore, 27, 45,
   47-49
and U.S. bombing
   cities, 51-52, 55
and Washington Naval
   Conference, 24
and WW I, 34
and WW II, 8, 10, 38-
   39, 41-53. *See also*
   Midway, Battle of
Java Sea, Battle of the, 50

Kaga, 57, 78-79, 80

Kakuta, 87
Katsumi, Motomi, 90
Kobayashi, Michio, 80, 81
Kondo, Nobutake, 57, 87, 88, 89, 90
Korea, 21-22
Kurita, Takeo, 89, 90
Kusaka, Ryunosuke, 72-73, 79

League of Nations, 34
Lend-Lease Act, 38
Leslie, Max, 78
Lexington, 53, 59
Liaotung Peninsula, 21
Lindsey, Gene, 74

MacArthur, Douglas, 42, 43-45
McClusky, Wade, 73, 77, 78, 79
Mahan, A.T., 32, 33
Maine, 29
Malaya, 27, 41, 43, 45-49
Manchuria
    and Japan, 21, 22, 25, 32-33, 35
    and United States, 32
Manifest Destiny, 30
Mao Zedong, 25
Meiji, 19-20, 22
Midway, Battle of
    and Battle of the Coral Sea, 12-13
    beginning of, 65-75
    dates for, 14, 65, 66
    and destruction of Japanese aircraft carriers, 57, 62, 77-85, 87-88, 89, 90, 92, 93-94, 95
    ending of, 92
    and first Japanese assault, 66-69

and first U.S. assault, 66-67, 68, 69
impact of, 95
and Japanese attack on Aleutian Islands, 11, 56, 57, 66, 87, 93
and Japanese casualties, 92
and Japanese coordinated attack, 69-73, 75
as Japanese defeat, 92-93
and Japanese navy, 56-57, 60, 62-63
and Japanese patrol planes, 68, 69-71, 75, 92
and Japanese planes, 57, 62, 67-68, 69-70, 92
Japanese preparation for, 56-58, 62-63
Japanese strategy for, 10-12, 13, 55-58, 93
and Japanese victories, 66-69, 70, 73-75, 90-92, 93
preparation for, 55-63
and retreat of Japanese fleet, 88-90
and sinking of *Yorktown,* 90-92
start of, 57, 63
as turning point in Pacific, 87-95
and U.S. casualties, 68, 91, 92
U.S. cracking Japanese code for, 12-15, 58, 65, 66, 93
and U.S. navy, 56, 57, 58-59, 60-62
and U.S. planes, 59-60, 61-62, 68, 70, 92

U.S. preparation for, 58-62, 63
U.S. strategy for, 15, 58-59, 61
and U.S. strike on Japanese invasion convoy, 66, 67
and U.S. successes, 75, 77-85, 87-92
as U.S. victory, 93-95
Midway Islands, 8
    See also Midway, Battle of
Mikuma, 89, 90
MI Operation, 57
Mogami, 89, 90

Nagumo, Chuichi, 56, 57, 63, 66-73, 74, 75, 77, 79, 80, 87, 88, 89, 90, 92-93, 95
Nanking, Rape of, 26, 43
Nimitz, Chester W., 95
    and Aleutians, 66
    background of, 7-8
    and Battle of Midway, 58-59, 60, 61, 66, 70
    and Battle of the Coral Sea, 12-13
    as commander of U.S. Pacific Fleet, 7-9
    and Pearl Harbor, 8

Open Door policy, 32-33, 35
O'Sullivan, John L., 30

Pearl Harbor
    Japanese attack on, 8, 10, 24, 35, 36-37, 95
    U. S. base at, 24, 35, 36-37
Percival, Arthur, 48
Perry, Matthew, 17-19

Philippines
    and Japan, 8-9, 41, 42,
        43-45
    and United States,
        29-30, 32, 35
Port Arthur, 21, 22
Port Darwin, 9
Port Moresby, 12-13,
    52-53
Puerto Rico, 30

Rochefort, Joseph, 12, 13
Roosevelt, Franklin
    Delano, 35-36, 38,
        39, 44
Roosevelt, Theodore,
    33-34
Russia, 21-23
Russo-Japanese War,
    21-23

Shannon, Harold, 59
Shoho, 53
Simard, Cyril T., 59, 65
Singapore, 27, 45, 47-49
Sino-Japanese War, 25-26,
    32, 42
Soryu, 57, 79-80
Spanish-American War,
    29-30
Spruance, Raymond A.,
    60, 62, 73, 74, 82, 84,
    88, 89, 92, 94-95
Sun Yat-sen, 25
Sweeney, Walter, 66, 70

Taiwan, 21
Tanabe, Yahachi, 90-92

Tanikaze, 90
Tojo, Hideki, 38, 42, 45,
    50
Tomonaga, Joichi, 67, 69,
    71, 82-83
Tsushima Straits, Battle
    of, 22

United States
    and Battle of the Coral
        Sea, 53
    and bombing Japanese
        cities, 51-53, 55
    and China, 30-31, 32,
        34, 35, 36
    and Hawaii, 31-32
    and isolation after
        WW I, 34, 35, 36
    and Manchuria, 32
    and Navy, 33-37, 52-53,
        56
    and Open Door policy,
        32-33, 35
    and Pearl Harbor
        attack, 8, 10, 38-39, 95
    and Pearl Harbor base,
        24, 35, 36-37
    and Perry in Japan,
        17-19
    and Philippines, 29-30,
        32, 35
    and planes, 51-52, 53
    and as power in
        Pacific, 29-33
    and Spanish-American
        War, 29-30
    and Washington Naval
        Conference, 24

    and WW I, 34, 35
    and WW II, 36-38,
        51-53. See also
        Midway, Battle of
    See also Nimitz,
        Chester W.

Wainwright, Jonathan,
    43, 45
Wake, 8
Waldron, John, 74
Wanghia, Treaty of, 30
Washington Naval
    Conference, 24
Wilson, Woodrow, 34
World War I, 34, 35
World War II
    beginning of, 26-27,
        36-37
    and Japan, 8, 10, 38-39,
        41-53. See also
        Midway, Battle of

Yamaguchi, Tamon, 72,
    80, 85
Yamamoto, Isoroku,
    9-12, 13, 55-58, 62, 66,
    80, 87-88, 89, 90, 92,
    93, 95
Yamashita, Tomoyuki,
    43, 46, 48-49
Yamato, 10, 87
Yanigimoto, Ryusaku,
    79-80
Yorktown, 53, 59, 60-62,
    66, 74, 78, 80-82, 83,
    90-92

page:

2:	Reprinted from S.L. Mayer (ed): *The Japanese War Machine,* Bison Books Limited, 1976, Distributed by The Hamlyn Publishing group Limited, Middlesex, England	46:	Associated Press, AP
		49:	Hulton Archive by Getty Images
		52:	Hulton Archive by Getty Images
		54:	© Corbis
		58:	Associated Press, AP
6:	Hulton Archive by Getty Images	61:	Hulton Archive by Getty Images
9:	© Bettmann/Corbis	64:	Hulton Archive by Getty Images
11:	Associated Press, AP	67:	© Corbis
14:	Associated Press, AP	71:	© Corbis
16:	© Bettmann/Corbis	76:	Associated Press, AP
22:	© Bettmann/Corbis	81:	Hulton Archive by Getty Images
26:	Associated Press, AP	84:	Reprinted from S.L. Mayer (ed): *The Japanese War Machine,* Bison Books Limited, 1976, Distributed by The Hamlyn Publishing group Limited, Middlesex, England
28:	Hulton Archive by Getty Images		
33:	Hulton Archive by Getty Images		
37:	© Christel Gerstenberg/Corbis		
39:	© Corbis		
40:	Hulton Archive by Getty Images	86:	© Bettmann/Corbis
44:	Hulton Archive by Getty Images	94:	Hulton Archive by Getty Images

cover: © Bettmann/Corbis

frontis: Reprinted from *The Japanese War Machine,* S.L. Mayer, ed.

RICHARD WORTH has thirty years experience as a writer, trainer, and video producer. He has written more than 25 books, including *The Four Levers of Corporate Change*, a best-selling business book. Many of his books are for young adults on topics that include family living, foreign affairs, biography, history, and the criminal justice system.